KUMBAYAH
THE JUNTEENTH STORY

A PLAY BY
ROSE MCGEE

INTRODUCTION BY
QADI MAHMOUD EL-KATI

WITH GENEROUS SUPPORT FROM

PUBLISHED BY

BELFREYBOOKS.

First Printing of Completely Revised Second Edition Copyright © 2015
by Rose McGee

Original Story Copyright © 1996 and
First Publication 1998 by Rose McGee

Published by Belfrey Books

For information contact:

BELFREY BOOKS
275 East 4th Street Suite 400
Saint Paul, MN 55101

belfreybooksllc@gmail.com

Printed in the United States of America

Publisher's Cataloging-in-Publication data
McGee, Rose

Kumbayah...the juneteenth story: a play in two acts / by Rose McGee –
Completely rev. 2nd ed.
p. cm.

ISBN 978-0-9836504-5-4

ADDITIONAL ACCOLADES

The play, Kumbayah...the Juneteenth Story teaches a significant part of U.S. history. I learned that the search for freedom resides in everyone's soul. Whether it is a freedom releasing one from persecution or simply a personal discovery.

—Shoshana Sagner, Saint Paul Academy and Summit School, Class of 2000

We often think that we have a firm grasp on knowledge, only to find out that what we know isn't anywhere near the full story. This was my experience after reading Rose McGee's Kumbayah...The Juneteenth Story. The absent narratives found in this story gave me a greater sense of pride in what our ancestors endured in their pursuits of freedom.

—Elmer Crumbley, Retired Principal, Omaha Public Schools

Throughout the years, the production has been touched by the community and an outpour of youth performers who have been fortunate enough to grow up with its rich message.

—*Insight News*

OTHER WORKS BY ROSE MCGEE

Anthologies
Chocolate Sweet Potato Pie Story, 2011
  (Saint Paul Almanac)

Can't Nobody Make A Sweet Potato Pie Like My Mama,
2010 *(Saint Paul Almanac)*
  http://saintpaulalmanac.org/saint-paul-stories/recipes/
  sweet-potato-pie/

Non-Fiction
Story Circle Stories, 2015 (Co-Author Ann Fosco)

Plays
Kumbayah...The Juneteenth Story, 1998, 2001, 2015

Sleep With A Virgin...A Perspective On AIDS, 2003

What About Me?, 1997

Since The Beginning, 1995(Co-Author Donna Glennie)

Poetry
Sleep With A Virgin...A Perspective On AIDS, 2001

Seriously Incorporated, 1989

And Then I Felt, 1979

Other Works by Rose McGee Continued

Publisher
Day by Day, 1996 (Written by Eden Women House)

Tedx Talk
The Power of Pie, 2011

DEDICATION

To Nana Barimba Kodwo Eduakwa
Chief of the Village of Atonkwa
and
To all the people (my new family)
who live in the Village of Atonkwa

With love and admiration
Adwoa Mansa

Visual Images

Original Paintings by Christopheraaron Deanes:
- *Praying Hands* – Oil, Gesso, Rice on Wood (*cover, p. 1*)
- *All to Thee* – Oil, Gesso, Rice on Wood (*p. 13*)
- *To The Hills* – Oil, Gesso, Rice on Wood (*p. 52*)

Youth Artist:
- *Freedom's Promise* by Angel Stock – Colored Pencils (*p. 114*) Blackburn High School Graduate; Metro Community College, Omaha, NE

Photographs Courtesy of:
- Steven Christopher Davis – 2009 Production (*p.131, 137, 140-147*)
- Reprinted by permission *Minneapolis Star Tribune:*
    - Qadi Mahmoud El-Kati, Renee Jones Schneider, Photographer © 2013 (*p. xiii*)
    - Robert "Bobby" Hickman, Jerry Holt, Photographer © 2005 (*p.151*)

Ghanaian Images:
- Kente Cloth (*p. 17*)
- Asante Stool – *Nyansapo* (Wisdom Knot) (*p. vii*)
- Asante Stool – *Crossed Swords* (Reigning Power) (*p. 149*)

MUSIC

Original Scores by Ben Mboya Ward:
- a. *Love Will Be A Bridge*
- b. *Freedom, Freedom*

Other:

Kumbaya (Gullah meaning "Come by Here"), A Gullah spiritual circa 1920s.

She'll Be Coming 'Round the Mountain (Based on an old Negro spiritual *When the Chariots Come*), circa late 1800s.

Battle Hymn of Republic (melody), William Steffe, 1856.

Hambone (Juba song – meaning slapping, stomping, dance, chanting), late 1850s.

FOREWORD

Photo courtesy of *Minneapolis Star Tribune*

By Qadi Mahmoud El-Kati

Among the most remarkable events drawn from the rich tapestry of the history of African people travail in Colonial and U.S. history is Juneteenth - Emancipation, the celebration of freedom from slavery. Critical students of history know that the celebration of Juneteenth is a chronologically misplaced holiday. *The Emancipation Proclamation* was issued by President Abraham Lincoln on January 1, 1863. This document signified the beginning of the official end of color/caste oppression on the part of the United States government.

The treachery of the slave-holding class who hid the knowledge of freedom from the enslaved combined to prevent their knowing of their supposed freedom until June of 1865 - over two and a half years after Lincoln's proclamation - which was just that - a proclamation. The official and legal halt to the institution of "Negro" enslavement did not occur until the Congress of the United States added the 13th Amendment to *The Constitution* in February of 1865. Juneteenth is in some ways, yet another metaphor that images for us the very complex career of American democracy, its arrogance of power, inhumanity, immorality, and living-death that we find in its midst. All revolved and revolves to this day around the thing that was euphemistically called "the peculiar institution."

The play, *Kumbayah...The Juneteenth Story* is skillfully penned by the mind, spirit and soothing creativity of the playwright, Rose McGee. She offered a window to look through and a frog's eye view of that sordid world. With deftness rarely equaled, she spins a bold episode of a people's will to endure, in spite of the world. With wondrous imagination, she has spawned a story which tells us what good stories mean, and what they are for and that is: a good tale deserves to be told over and over again - across the generations. Beneath the terror of ugliness that was slavery, and indeed its aftermath, we discover people in all of their human weight and complexity – feeling, dreaming, crying and laughing, being funny and sad, melancholy and hopeful, and poised to struggle.

The unexpected and clever deceive of springing *Kumbayah's* drama from the placement of our youth in a contemporary urban setting – a restaurant – "makes it real", and "back in the day" a part of this day. Intergenerational construction of material for the stage drama may very well become a standard in transmitting central ideas, information, values of historical sensibilities to our young. In today's life and times, the stuff of history, which is the study of continuity and change, is difficult to gauge. We live in a media buttressed by a deliberate system to mis-educate the populace. *The Lies My Teacher Told Me* has made huge contribution to the confused madness over the meaning and value of history. One thing is certain, history produces everything, which is why "*everything is everything.*"

Rose McGee delineates a fast-paced and impressive collage of characters who offer dramatic and plausible images of members of America's enslaved population. These characters have complex fates and are thoroughly human and spiritual, while grounded in a harsh world of inhumanity. *Lewis* and *Florence* show the power of love and its strange flights and capacity to dream. The ability to dream is what makes us human. *Angus* and *Wade* are two mindless representatives of the landed gentry and the arrogance that is married to power. *Yaa Asantewaa* portrays the mysticism that so often colors the African sense of being. There is the undercurrent connection between *Professor Mankata* and *Yaa Asantewaa*. And of course, the flux of indecisiveness on the part of *Abe Lincoln* and the well-known assertiveness of *Mary Todd Lincoln*, who sometimes would brow-beat her husband. *Frederick Douglass* as *Narrator* and conscience is a perfectly placed voice. All of this, and more, challenges the uneasy American imagination with an undaunted, un-Hollywood view of plantation life. The resilience of this community is conspicuous, with its many characters of will. Philosophers have called such stuff "the human spirit."

The event in Texas which led to black Texans' appellation and observance of Emancipation Day, six months removed, is owed to improbable circumstances, as in so much of human history. Juneteenth is now an honored occasion. There is little doubt from this quarter, that the artist who is in the generality, far ahead of the rest of society in thought and vision, will quite possibly lead in nudging us to understand and appreciate our national history in a different light.

The daring pen of Rose McGee asserts that theatrical space and unhampered technique can be used (better than textbooks) to make history not only entertaining and educational, but also inspiration, by a spirit that says, "yes" to life! The drab and shop-worn images of kings, queens, courts, generals, wars, treaties, edicts and peace pacts, and lifeless most "significant dates" can be replaced, or at least recast with drama that transcends politics and ideology.

There is a great amount of useful social history in this play. The almost naturalistic integration of the great musical heritage of African Americans with drama amounts to minor stroke of genius. *Kumbayah...The Juneteenth* Story itself is a song, sung and acted from the classical oral tradition of black peoples' music. It is here that the playwright acts as orchestrator of the form and function of black American culture. It is culture that has for so long been a persistent, creative and powerful force in what we are pleased to call popular American culture. "*Body Talk*", which is dance and music, spirit with voice first, is a notoriously religious value in the context of African culture everywhere. This principal is woven with dialogue in to the essence of African spirit - rhythm! There is magic and mystery! The play is a poem!

Thus far, Rose McGee, the accomplished poet, storyteller and now playwright, has introduced a gem in the making. It is a critical and suppressed chapter which needs exposure. It is the underside of United States history whose exposure is so necessary for the growth of this adolescent nation. This history, specifically the institution "Negro Slavery", the Civil War, Reconstruction and its overthrown, and its living extension commonly called the Civil Rights Movement, is what challenges democracy at this hour. The present is always informed by the past and the "past never passes". We need a gaggle of such historical keys put on the dramatic stage. Thanks, Rose. Stay well and stay the course.

Qadi Mahmoud El-Kati is Professor Emeritus, Macalester College in Saint Paul, Minnesota and served as historical consultant to Rose McGee in developing *Kumbayah...The Juneteenth Story*. He is highly regarded as an official griot and keeper of knowledge. Most importantly, he teachers people to understand the richness of self-identity as it connects to the beginning of all humanity...black awareness.

INTRODUCTION

By Rose McGee

WHY THIS STORY?

I was born and raised in the rural south – Jackson, Tennessee with my grandmother, great-grandmother, and lots of chatty old people. Yet I never heard of Juneteenth. Growing up, I spent each summer in Minneapolis, Minnesota with my father and met lots of talkative northerners...still never heard of Juneteenth. Even though I attended all-black schools, an

HBCU (Historically Black Colleges and Universities), and black churches (CME, AME, Baptist, COGC, etc.) it was not until after I graduated from Lane College and moved to Denver, Colorado that I became exposed to this pivotal point of history.

Not surprising! Turns out, a large population of African Americans living in Denver migrated from Texas. I tell you - they are to be commended for maintaining and passing on the story! This play was written to spread the word of the value of freedom and to help all ages understand the significance of emancipation for black people in this country.

WHY AFRICA?

NOTE: The words *Asante* and *Ashanti* are both used to describe the people, the region, and the sacred stool of unity. *Asante* is the original word used by the Ghanaians. *Ashanti* was coined by whites when the African Nation became colonized by the British. Throughout my writings and within the script, I will use the word *Asante* as was the language of the indigenous.

As a result of having met world renowned visual artist, Dr. John T. Biggers in 1996, I was somewhat familiar with various Adinkra symbols of the Akan culture – Ghana, West Africa. Dr. Biggers had spent time in Minneapolis mentoring local emerging artists in designing "The Celebration of Life" mural. The magnificent images of large washing/cooking pots, the sankofa bird, and the Asante stools were painted on an Olson Memorial Highway sound barrier in the heart of North Minneapolis. After traveling home to the *Motherland* of Africa in December 1997 and again in July 1999, I became extremely fascinated with the history of the Asante Kingdom located in Ghana. Inspiration was abound as I began weaving in aspects of the *real* Africa - the traditions, the people, and storytelling into the play. In doing so, I was implanting a stronger sense of value and respect within my *own* being.

The Asante Nation was mighty in battle and believed wholeheartedly that the *Golden Asante Stool* kept the souls of their people in "unity." I became especially driven by the story of *Nana Yaa Asantewaa*, Queen Mother of Edweso located near Kumasi, and felt compelled to incorporate her into the script. Such a tiny woman she was, yet when the sacred *Golden Asante Stool* was in jeopardy of being stolen by the British, she led an Asante army into battle. During the character's appearance in the play, she wears the royal yellow kente cloth. This story demonstrates that despite centuries of persecution – black people who were uprooted from their homes, dismantled from their families then plopped on continents way across what must have seemed like endless waters – still their souls remained in unity. With such a strong tie, 'tis no wonder the spirit of freedom will never be broken.

My apologies to those who speak *Twi (a common language spoken by people who live in Kumasi)*. In the script, you will notice that our computers lack the proper fonts needed for typing each symbol or icon – but it is the intent that counts.

WHAT IS THE PROCESS?

Everything begins in *circle*. When cast convenes as a group for the first time, the script is read while sitting in circle. This is so important because in Minnesota, most of our diverse cast had never heard of Juneteenth prior to their involvement with the production. Some were familiar with the park festivities and the parades, but had no idea of the purpose for the celebration. Before each performance, the cast stands together on stage (in circle) in order to become centered and focused. The play's purpose goes beyond acting…it extends into educating, learning, mentoring, and telling an important black history narrative that has deliberately been omitted from our social construct. As elders and raconteurs, our job is to pass it on so that youth will grab hold, grow from the knowledge, and remember to pass it on.

Youth in the production work with professional actors who mentor them on and off the set in a positive and safe environment. Just as the Director mentors a student assistant director, the musicians and dancers are comprised of both youth and adults. High school interns assisted me in the reading, typing and editing of the original book (script).

Everyone in the cast is taught to observe small details such as the different levels of dialect spoken by the captives and that ignorance is not always determined by the way a person speaks. *Lewis* has no formal education, but is brilliant and handles the white man's financial matters with perfection. Had he been a white man, *Lewis* would be very wealthy. *Florence* is obviously a quick study. Without being in a formal school setting, as a child she grasped literary bits and pieces fed to her as playmate to *Mastah Turner's* daughter.

Captives were trained and conditioned at birth to realize their station in life. Even though the black and white children are friends and play together (*Samuel, Luke, Daniel, Stuart, Alice* and the others), only the white children wear shoes and are always referred to as "Mastah" or "Miss" by the black children. However, "*Freedom is a spiritual situation. African people might have been chained and bound in shackles for almost 300 years, but some understood the meaning of true freedom and would not settle for less.*" (Douglass Act Two: Scene Two).

In January 1996, *Kumbayah ...The Juneteenth Story* began as a work in progress and was presented that June as an informal, audience engaged program that inched its way into play status by June of 1997. Both performances were held in Concordia University's E.M. Pearson Theatre in Saint Paul, Minnesota. In June 1998, the play opened in The Great American History Theatre downtown Saint Paul. Eventually, the Landmark Center's Weyerhaeuser Auditorium in Saint Paul became home for the play's annual production.

Reflective dialogues are key after each presentation. The interaction offers our audiences a chance to speak openly and establish among themselves evolving themes such as: freedom, justice, education, perseverance, courage, family, traditions, loyalty, etc. Many leave the production personally inspired to do something that will make a positive difference.

Like the production of *Kumbayah...The Juneteenth Story*, each dialogue confirms that acquiring equality and equity in this country remains an enormous work in progress!

WHY NOT FLIP THE SCRIPT?

NOTE: The term "community" refers to theater companies, schools, afterschool programs, colleges/universities, churches – whoever is doing this production.

There is a special uniqueness to this production. Scenes are intentionally created for producers to adapt the script to your community's own needs. Act One: Scene One is where community talent can be incorporated into the presentation. For example, one year we used a Hmong Hip Hop Dance group from Saint Paul to perform in the restaurant scene. The troupe had never heard of Juneteenth until the play. A large audience of Hmong parents came out to support their children. As a result, everyone learned something new from each other. One year a group of African American tumblers from the Beacons' afterschool program in Minneapolis performed. In addition to the newly acquired knowledge of Juneteenth, it was an incredible experience for those students because most had never traveled to Saint Paul (only fifteen to twenty minutes away from Minneapolis).

Here's something fun – several scenes are interchangeable. Therefore, you may replace the script depending upon which story you want to convey. In the first publication, I wrote in the characters, *Abraham Lincoln* and *Mary Todd Lincoln*. Over the years, I decided to switch it up a bit and created *Lincoln's Servants* and deleted the *Lincolns*. While cleaning up Lincoln's office, two servants, *Uncle Earl* (an elderly black man) and *Leroy* (younger black man who knows how to read) become the focus. The two stumble across words written on trashed papers which is a draft of Lincoln's *Emancipation Proclamation*. Since both versions have been received very well by audiences, I decided to include the two in this edition. If you have time for a longer performance, both scenes can be performed.

Blind casting works beautifully in this prodution. One year, a young girl auditioned and seemed perfect as *Samuel*, so I flipped the character to *Samuella*. It was such a hit, *Samuella* replaced *Samuel* for at least three years. Another time, I decided to allow *Reverend Cleo* to deliver the news of freedom to the plantation slaves instead of having *General Gordon Granger* read it. Again, if you have time for a longer version, both scenes can be performed.

If you are fortunate enough to have access to an authentic African drum and dance troupe in your community, this production is a great way to partner. In Act Two: Scene One as *Mama* is telling *Florence* the story of how her husband (*Florence's* father) had been stolen as a young boy (*Son* in Prologue) from his home in Africa. Their conversation continues as the women exit off-stage. Enters the African drum and dance troupe re-enacting the courtship in a way that takes the audience back into time when the <u>parents</u> of *Florence's* father meet. Makes sense, for in the Prologue we have witnessed the strong love between the two before *Mother* and *Son* are abducted. Meanwhile, you now have a full performance of authentic and powerful energy incorporated into the play.

After the play concludes, this is an excellent opportunity for reflective dialogue. Invite a community leader or celebrity to facilitate the discussion. The cast comes out, is introduced, sits on the stage, and responds to questions presented by the facilitator. Afterwards open up to the audience for additional questions and comments. What's just as powerful is when the cast asks a few questions of the audience. This engagement allows everyone to learn from each other and it also helps feed content into your next production. Just as social justice and change are infinite, this story will never be complete, but simply: *Stepped on a pin, the pin bent and that's the way the story went.*

SHORT SYNOPISIS

KUMBAYAH...THE JUNETEENTH STORY

The play, *Kumbayah ...The Juneteenth Story* is a 90 to 120-minute fictional, two-act production that addresses a factual and traumatic event - the rape of emancipation against African people who were held as captives in the United States. Storytelling and music weave together unforgettable episodes. Although tragedy is depicted, this play within a play is tremendously uplifting. Featured is original music written by Ben Mboya Ward – *Love Will Find A Way* and *Freedom, Freedom.* (*soundtrack available upon request from publisher*). For daytime school audiences, no Intermission. For evening and weekend matinees, a 15-minute Intermission is suggested after Act One. **Optional**: Noted scenes can be interchangeable or all-inclusive. The latter extends production to 120 minutes.

The story begins with a Prologue set in the early 1800s in a small West African village where a young mother and her small son are being abducted from their home by slave catchers. Act One: Scene One is set in present time in a popular North Minneapolis soul-food restaurant where a group of youth and adults ultimately end up discussing what *Juneteenth* means. Before long they all have agreed to go "across the river" (the Mississippi) to Saint Paul and attend a play on the subject of Juneteenth. The story then shifts into historical era on the *Turner Plantation* in Tyler, Texas with the character *Frederick Douglass* as *Narrator*. Several roles are portrayed by the same actors (intentionally).

Our super hero *Lewis*, is a brilliant young slave who is about to turn twenty-one years old – at which time his white owner, *Ole Mastah Turner* (who we never see throughout the play) has promised him his freedom as a birthday present. *Lewis* is in love with the lovely *Florence*, also a slave, and plans to buy her freedom and marry her. While on a cattle-selling trip in Galveston, Texas for the ailing *Mastah Turner*, *Lewis* learns that President Abraham Lincoln has freed the slaves. As he returns to the plantation, exuberant over the news of freedom, *Lewis* is stopped by *Pattyrollers* (slave catchers). Since *Lewis* knows the guarded secret, fatality becomes inevitable. Over the next two and a half years, Lewis' mythical spirit (perhaps interpreted by devout storytellers as *John De Conqueror*) soars over the earth and through the skies as an *eagle* serving as a "protector" to his people. Word of freedom finally gets delivered to the captives on June 19, 1865 via *General Gordon Granger's* arrival in Texas issuing the mandate. Thus the term *Juneteenth*.

THE FIRST FULL PRODUCTION:

KUMBAYAH...THE JUNETEENTH STORY

A PLAY BY ROSE MCGEE

Directed by
James A. Williams and W. Toni Carter

Assistant Director: Roslyn Harmon
Stage Manager: Mary Kay Orman
Music Director: Ben Mboya Ward
Dance Choreographer: Stephan Reynolds
Set Designer: Patrick Cunningham
Lighting Designer: Mitchell Frazier
Editor: Alanna Carter

Kumbayah ...The Juneteenth Story

The Great American History Theatre – June 1998
Saint Paul, Minnesota

THE CAST:

Swipe, Lewis.. Melvin Carter, III
KaTeshia, Florence .... Tenniece Nesbit
Frederick Douglass .... Robert (Bobby) Hickman
Nate .... Metric Giles
Brenda, Mary Todd Lincoln .... Laurel Orman
Samuel .... Adam Davis-McGee
Granger, Pattyroller #1 .... Myron Greenberg
Daniel .... Kyle Ingleman
Professor Mankata, Yaa Asantewaa .... Antoinette Adjeia
Luke, Teller .... Arne Gjelten
Abby, Teller .... Stacy Wilson
Waitress, Mama .... Mari Harris
Alice .... Jacob Trotzky-Sirr
Angus .... Jesse Kanson-Benanav
Stuart .... Sam Kanson-Benanav
Teller, Child #1 .... Isaiah Ellison
Teller, Child #2 .... Jeremiah Ellison
Teller, Child #3 .... Jazzalette Wandrick
Teller, Child #4 .... Jocelyn Hill
Ancestor Child .... Jeremy McGee
Ancestor Child .... Andrea Giles
Writer/Co-Producer .... Rose McGee
Co-Producer. .... W. Toni Carter
Director .... James A. Williams
Assistant Director .... Roslyn Harmon
Dance Choreographer .... Stephen Reynolds
Stage Manager .... Mary Kay Orman
Historical Consultant .... Mahmoud El-Kati

MUSICIANS:

Music Director .... Ben Mboya Ward
Vocalist...Mari Harris
Trumpet...Gene Adams
Flutist .... Frank Wharton
Drummer... Wilbert Dugas
Bass Guitar..Aaron James

DANCERS/AFRICAN DRUMMERS:

Nimely Napla and The Nimely Pan African Dance
Company
Stephan Reynolds and Kimberly Madry

SET TECHNICIAN/ARTIST/LIGHTS:

Set Design ....Patrick Cunningham
Light Designer ....Mitchell Frazier

KUMBAYAH . . . THE JUNTEENTH STORY
A PLAY BY ROSE MCGEE

SET DESIGN

TIME PERIODS:
1. West Africa early 1800s
2. Present Day (1998)
3. Texas and Washington D.C. 1863 to 1865

SETTINGS:
Note: A tree stomp or an Asante Stool remain on stage and visible in every scene to symbolically connect the past with the present.

- **African Outdoors**: Vegetables, straw.
- **Restaurant**: Three to four tables; enough chairs for cast; counter with stools nice to add; menus, door chime. If real food is used – chicken wings only; although red punch is mentioned – avoid due to possible spills and stains on costumes.
- **Outdoor/Plantation Yard**: Trees, rocks for the outdoors; tree stump.
- **Dark Rural Wooded Area**: Trees, vines, rocks for the outdoors.
- **Lincoln's Study**: One executive looking chair, desk, feathered quill, balled up papers; tea pot, two tea cups.

BACKDROP:
Slides can be used to reflect historical scenes of African life, plantation life, the authentic Emancipation Proclamation and General Gordon Granger's General Order #3.

ITEMS:
Painted theater cubes can be used to depict items such as: rocks, Adinkra symbols, tree stumps, traditional African symbols such as a three-legged cooking/wash pot, an Asante stool; images of bondage (chains, a tree); images of freedom (wings, birds). A variety of African textiles and prints.

AUDITORIUM:
Center and side aisles are kept clear for exits and entrances of characters.

Cast Of Characters:

PROLOGUE:

HUSBAND: Black man, early twenties.

MOTHER: Black woman, early twenties.

SON: Black boy, 8 to 10 years old. Can be Historical character – *Ancestor Child or Child teller*.

SLAVE
CATCHER #1: White male, early twenties to middle age. Can be Historical character *Wade* or *Angus* (if Scenes used can be *Granger* or *Lincoln*).

SLAVE
CATCHER #2: White male, early twenties to middle age. Can be Historical character *Wade* or *Angus* (if Scenes used can be *Granger* or *Lincoln*).

PRESENT DAY CHARACTERS:

KATESHIA: Black girl, mid-to-late teens, smart, little to no tolerance for nonsense. Also plays Historical character *Florence*.

BRENDA: Black girl, mid-to-late teens, wealthy, although not as uptight – best friend to *KaTeshia*, somewhat naïve. Also plays Historical character *Abby*.

WAITRESS: Black woman, middle-aged, friendly, busy-body. Also plays Historical character *Mama*.

REVEREND
CLEO: Black male, middle age, outgoing, sermonic/storyteller. Plays Historical character *Reverend Cleo*.

DEACON: Black male, middle to older age, friend to *Reverend Cleo*, enjoys being in the midst of excitement. Plays Historiccal character *Lincoln's Servant, Uncle Earl*.

CHILD #1: Black boy, 8 to 12, high energy, inquisitive. Plays Historical character *Samuel*.

CHILD #2: Black girl, 8 to 12, high energy, intelligent, inquisitive. Plays Historical character *Alice*.

CHILD #3: White boy, 8 to 12, very quiet, somewhat mischievous. Plays Historical character *Luke*.

NATE:

Black male, late teens to early twenties, intellectual, very outgoing, meets no strangers. Also plays Historical character *Lincoln's Servant, Leroy.*

SWIPE:

Black male, late teens to early twenties, intellectual, down to earth, reserved. Also plays Historical character *Lewis.*

PROFESSOR
ADWOA
MANKATA:

Black woman, late twenties to middle age, African-born accent, intelligent, serious, yet appreciates humor. Also plays Historical character *Yaa Asantewaa.*

HISTORICAL CHARACTERS:

FREDERICK
DOUGLASS:

Black male, middle to older age, distinguished, serves as *Narrator.*

LEWIS:

Black male, late teens to early twenties, strong sense for business, wisdom, in love with *Florence*, has no blood relatives. Also plays Present Day character *Swipe.*

FLORENCE:

Black girl, mid-to-late teens, in love with *Lewis*, knowledge seeker, daughter to *Mama* and *Samuel's* older sister. Same actor as Present Day character *KaTeshia.* Must be a vocalist for two solos.

MAMA:

Middle aged black woman, *Florence* and *Samuel's* mother, hard worker, protector of the children, same actor as Present Day character *Waitress.*

GENERAL
GORDON
GRANGER: Older white male, authoritative, committed to giving and carrying out orders as deemed necessary. NOTE: Optional depending on whether Scene is used. Same actor as Historical character *Pattyroller #1 or #2*.

ABRAHAM
LINCOLN: Older white male, distinguished, tormented. NOTE: Optional depending whether Scene is used. Same actors as Historical character *Pattyroller #1 or #2*.

WADE
TURNER: White male, late teens to early twenties, son of *Turner Plantation* owner, jealous of *Lewis'* trusted position on the plantation and of his relationship with *Florence*. Same actor as Prologue *Slave Catcher #1 or #2*.

ANGUS
FULLER: White male, late teens to early twenties, son of *Fuller Plantation* owner, friend to *Wade*, gullible and easily led by *Wade*. Same actor as Prologue *Slave Catcher #1 or #2*.

SAMUEL: Black boy, 8 to 12 years old, Florence's younger brother, somewhat mischievous. Plays Present Day character *Child #1*.

ALICE:

Black girl, 8 to 12 years old, rough as the boys, lives on Turner Plantation. Plays Present Day character *Child #2*.

DANIEL:

Black boy, 8 to 12 years old, cousin and friend to *Samuel*, somewhat mischievous, *Abby's* younger brother.

LUKE
TURNER:

White boy, 8 to 12 years old, younger son of *Turner Plantation* owner, younger brother to *Wade*, friend to *Samuel*. Present Day character *Child #3*, friend to *Child #1* and *Child #2*.

STUART
FULLER:

White boy, 8 to 12 years old, friend to *Luke*, lives on the *Fuller Plantation* near the *Turner Plantation*, younger brother to *Angus*.

YAA
ASANTEWAA:

Black woman, late twenties to middle age, African-born accent, Ancestor who appears before *Lewis* as his "protector." Same actor as Present Day character *Professor Adwoa Mankata*.

ABBY:

Black girl, mid-to-late-teens, cousin to *Florence*, *Daniel's* older sister. Plays *Brenda* in Present Day Scene.

MARY TODD
LINCOLN:

Middle-aged white woman, married to *Lincoln*; oddly sympathetic to his agony.

PATTY-
ROLLER #1:   Any age white male, heavy drinker, heavy gambler. Can be one of the following: (a) If Scene is used, can be same actor as *Granger* or *Lincoln*. (b) If enough white actors, can also play *Slave Catcher* and *Pattyroller* (c) If not enough white actors, this Scene can be narrated by *Frederick Douglass* with *Ancestors* dancing.

PATTY-
ROLLER #2:   Same as above.

TELLERS
#1,#2,#3,#4:   Youth members of *Ensemble*. children of any ethnicity, 8 to 13.

ANCESTOR
CHILDREN: Youth members of *Ensemble*. children of any ethnicity, 8 to 13. Can also be *TELLERS #1, 2, 3, 4.*

LEAD
ANCESTOR
DANCER: Black male or woman. Must be a good modern and/or African dancer. Has two lead/solo dance scenes.

CHILD
ANCESTOR
DANCERS: Four black youth and other ethnicities; male and female dancers ages 8 and up.

LIVE MUSIC: Piano keyboardist; African drummer; other instrumentalists of choice. Must learn two original *Love Will Be A Bridge* and *Freedom, Freedom* by Ben Mboya Ward.

PROLOGUE

STAGE: CURTAINS DRAWN.

TIME: Small Village in West Africa early 1800s.

MUSIC: Upbeat African music – drums, other instruments. Music continues for about 30 seconds.

CURTAINS
OPEN: Scene is done in silence/pantomime.

SET: *Mother and Son already on stage.*

                   In a small village located in Ghana, West
                   Africa, a young *Mother* and her small *Son*
                   are harvesting fresh vegetables from their
                   garden. *Mother* is teaching *Son* how to
                   select items that are ripe and ready to be
                   harvested.

                   Husband Enters.

                   In preparing to leave for hunting, he sur-
                   prises his wife with a gift of two pieces
                   of lovely *kente* cloth. She wraps one on
                   her head and the other around her waist.
                   Gleeful expressions of appreciation are
                   exhibited. Soon the man extends goodbye
                   hugs to his wife and child. *Husband* exits
                   stage as *Mother* and *Son* remain on stage
                   in the garden. *Mother* resumes teaching
                   Son how to harvest. Occasionally she
                   pauses to admire the beautiful *kente* cloth.

MUSIC: Transitions into dramatic, tension tempo.

Slave Catchers Enter:

Lurking in the background are two *Slave Catchers* who sneak upon the defenseless woman and child, apprehend the pair, and drag them off stage.

(*Mother* makes audible scream) Amidst the struggle, the *kente* cloth around *Mother's* waist falls to the ground. (Music continues dramatically for about 10 seconds.)

Husband Enters:

Husband returns home with evidence of a successful hunt. He searches around for his wife and child, sees only spilled vegetables, then notices the *kente* cloth on the ground. When he realizes his family has been abducted, he falls to his knees, weeps. (*Husband* releases audible agonizing cry for about three seconds). A short while later, he rises, picks up his spear and charges off in search of his family.

MUSIC: Instruments rise louder, dramatic tempo.

CURTAINS
CLOSE: BLACKOUT.

Music plays for about 30 seconds allowing time to re-set stage for Act One: Scene One.

ACT ONE

ACT ONE

SCENE ONE

TIME: Week of June 19, 1998 (AKA Present Day).

PLACE: A popular soul-food restaurant in North Minneapolis, Minnesota.

MUSIC: Instrumental, contemporary upbeat; plays for one minute. Restaurant door chimes - enter *Brenda* and *KaTeshia* already engaged in conversation. Music fades out as conversation begins, girls proceed to center vacant table.

SET: When curtain rises, restaurant scene is in place; at least 3 tables; at least 9 chairs; kente cloth on floor is noticeable only to the audience; menus; open space for community performers. *KaTeshia, Brenda, Child #1, #2, #3* already seated at tables. Waitress busy taking orders and going back and forth waiting on customers. *KaTeshia* and *Brenda* and look intense. *Child #1, #2, #3* engaged in a book.

BRENDA: KaTeshia? What on Earth happened to your nails?

KATESHIA: Girl, I got'em done over on Broadway a-gain. But, I ain't never going back over there no more. (*busy inspecting her nails with great look of frustration and big-time attitude. Waitress comes to table with pad and pencil*)

WAITRESS: Welcome to Lucille's. May I take your orders?

KATESHIA: I'll have an order of chicken wings and a Zulu Punch.

BRENDA: (*Unfamiliar with this type of menu selections; unsure of what to order*) Pig feet? Oxtail Stew? Ah…I'll just have whatever she's having.

KATESHIA: I think I'll take a piece of corn bread, too.

BRENDA: Ah…me too. (*Waitress writes down orders as girls continue talking*)

KATESHIA: (*Speaking to Brenda*) Look at my fingers how infected they are. I put this purple polish on to try and cover up the fungus.

WAITRESS: (*Leans over and looks at KaTeshia's nails*) You musta got your nails done over on Broadway! Girl, that's why I ain't got no nails to-day!

(*Door chimes; Enter Rev. Cleo and Deacon*)

KATESHIA: I know that's right.

WAITRESS: Well, hello Rev. Cleo, Deacon.How y'all doing today?

REV. CLEO: Doing mighty fine, Sister. Doing mighty Fine.

CHILD #1: Rev. Cleo, I heard your wife was one of the finalists in the sweet potato pie contest that Deep Roots Desserts is putting on. Congratulations!

REV. CLEO: Oh yes! Without a doubt, she does Louisiana proud. (*boastful, jovial*) Woman knows she can make a mean sweet potato pie! That's how she hooked me, you know. I had one slice of her pie and the next thing I knew I was standing at the altar saying, "I do." (*All laugh*)

CHILD #1: (*Boastful*) Well…I'm the lucky one. I get to be one of the judges for the final taste. Emmmmm...I can't wait!

CHILD #2: Lucky You!

CHILD #1: You got that right! I hear there are some good tasting pies in that contest.

WAITRESS: Just have a seat right over there, gentlemen and I'll be right with you. (*Rev. Cleo and Deacon get seated; Waitress steps away to handle another business*)

BRENDA: Sweet potato pie? (*Puzzled*) That's like pumpkin pie, right?

WAITRESS: (*Cuts into conversation*). Girl please! Sweet potato pie has more soul than pumpkin!

DEACON: Ain't no comparison!

REV. CLEO: That's mighty right! Matter of fact, I consider it to be the "sacred" dessert of our culture.

WAITRESS: It's sacred alright. Everybody thinks "their" Mama makes the best sweet potato pie.

ALL: That's right! (*All laugh*)

REV. CLEO: You know. I believe I feel a sermon coming on.

CHILD #2: (*With warning*) Uhhh, Oooh!

REV. CLEO: (*Jumps up from his seat and begins to walk towards the audience. Begins to speak in a preacher, call and response style*) I said. I believeeeee I feel a sermon coming on. And it's all about that sacred!

ALL: Sacred!

REV. CLEO: That saaaaaaaaaay-cred!

ALL: Saaaaaaaaaa-cred!

REV. CLEO:	Sweet potato pie.
ALL:	Yes! (*Rev. Cleo breaks into a sanctified dance; music starts*)
WAITRESS:	Rev. Cleo! (*Attempting to calm him down; he continues; she speaks louder*). REV. CLEO! REV. CLEO!
REV. CLEO:	(*Comes back to reality; music stops*) Ah! Ah! Yes, Sister!
WAITRESS:	Can you just hold off on that sermon until I take your order?
	(*Rev. Cleo laughs and returns to his seat next to Deacon*)
CHILD #1:	Never know what you'll see up in here. (*Speaking softly to Child # 2 and Child #3; all laughing; door chimes*)
KATESHIA:	(*Turns attention toward the door as Nate and Swipe enter*) Oooh, Girl don't look now, but two Denzel Washington wanna-be's just strolled up in here. I tell you! Some people!
NATE:	Hey! Whut up La-dies? (*Flirtatious*)
SWIPE:	Ump! (*Somewhat aloof; not altogether interested*)
NATE:	Y'all live over North?

BRENDA: (*Appears a bit nervous. Feeling somewhat out of her element*) Well…Ah…No, I live in Edina.

NATE: (*Moves in closer to Brenda*) EDINA! That's where all the rich white folks live. Girl, what you doing up in here then! Just kidding. My name is Nate and this is my main man, Swipe.

SWIPE: Uh-huh! (*Not really focusing on their conversation*)

KATESHIA: Can't he talk? (*Annoyed by Swipe's dismissive attitude*)

NATE: Sure he can talk. He's just an in-te-lect-u-al (*Plays with the word*) kind of guy of few words. (*Takes her response as an invitation, pulls out a chair sits down with the girls. Swipe's already studying, remains where seated*) So, you la-dies be going to the Juneteenth Festival Sunday over at Wirth Park?

BRENDA: (*Still uncomfortable, but interested*) Well…Ah…

KATESHIA: …Undecided. (*Gives Nate a quick brush-off; notices Swipe's into the books*)

NATE: How 'bout we jess hang out with y'all over there, then? (*Waitress returns with the girls' orders*)

WAITRESS: That sounds like a good id…

KATESHIA: …I don't think so. (*Gives waitress a "mind your own business" look*)

NATE: (*Not one to give up easily*) Well, y'all going to the Juneteenth Play, then? We got flyers if you need one.

WAITRESS: (*The ever-busy body*) I heard about that play on KMOJ…or was it KFAI? Well, maybe it was both.

KATESHIA: We got plans, don't we Brenda?

BRENDA: (*Puzzled - looks to KaTeshia, then to Nate*) What plans? What play? I don't even know what June-tenth is!

KATESHIA: (*Gives Brenda a "hush your mouth" look, then corrects her*) "Juneteenth!" Never mind, Brenda. (*turns to Nate*) We're busy. Now, if you don't mind we're about to eat our food.

NATE: No problem, we'll just order too.(*Turns his attention to the waitress*) I want me some of them wings and some red beans and rice. How 'bout you, man?

SWIPE: Um, huh. (*Never looks up from books, nods in agreement, Waitress writes down their orders*)

WAITRESS: (*Looks over Swipe's shoulder into his book*) Eman-ci-pa-tion Pro-cla-ma-tion … Huh! Ain't no emancipation from working on my feet serving chicken wings all day! Huh! (*Waitress exits in a huff*)

KATESHIA: I don't believe this! (*Girls begin eating their wings as Professor Adwoa Mankata enters and approaches Swipe*)

CHILD #1: I do! (*All three children laugh*)

SWIPE: (*First to notice her arrival*) Professor Mankata! (*Both Swipe and Nate stand. Swipe pulls out a chair for her to sit down*)

NATE: Whut's up Prof? You can sit here if you wanna.

MANKATA: (*Walks over to where Swipe is seated*) Hello. Yes, I will join you. Thank you. (*She takes a seat*)

NATE: You gotta try some of these chicken wings, Prof! They be smok'n! (*Points to the girls' plates*)

BRENDA: They sure are!

KATESHIA: (*With disgust, she addresses Nate*) "Prof?"

CHILD #3: "Be smok'n?" I need to check and see if that's in this new book I just got written by a (*Struggles with pronouncing author's name. Swipe becomes interested, gets up from seat and walks over to Children's table, looks over Child #3's shoulder and helps with pronouncing the name.*)

SWIPE: Mah-moud El-Ka-ti. (*Child #3 looks appreciative to Swipe*) You know about "The Hippionary?" We just attended Professor El-Kati's Book signing last week. Too cool. Ain't it man? (*Turns to Nate who nods in agreement*)

SPECIAL
NOTE: (*Door Chimes*)*This is where a local performance can be inserted such as a youth hip-hop group or a spoken word group – whatever Director and community decide to showcase. The Guest Artists enter restaurant to pick up a "to go" order. If it's SPOKEN WORD artists, then LANGUAGE becomes Waitress and Deacon's emphasis. If it's a dance, tumbling, step group, line-dance troupe, etc. then MOVEMENT becomes Waitress and Deacon's emphasis. When performance is over, Guest Artists get their "to go" order and exit stage.*

WAITRESS: (*Jumps into the conversation*) It's all about our language, our style, our movement with words. Child! Our moooove-ment in general YEAH! (*She makes a couple of hip hop moves*)

DEACON: Did somebody say "MOVEMENT?" (*Deacon begins making some hip-hop movements; Guest Artists jumps in to show him how it's really done; Deacon steps back. This can go on as a performance for about 2 to 3 minutes. Guest Artists perform for 2 to 3 minutes; when almost done, they pull Deacon back into the performance with them, let him do his thing; then Child #1, 2 and 3 get excited, jump up and join in. This goes for about 1 minute. At end of performance, Deacon appears physically exhausted. Rev. Cleo comes to his aid.*)

REV CLEO: Deacon! DEACON! Contain yo'self Deacon!

DEACON: (*Embarrassed, but happy*) Ah...Yes..Yes. I'm fine Reverend. I'm fine. (*Deacon returns to his seat; Children return to their seats; Guest Artists exit stage.*)

CHILD #3: Wow! You are right. (*Looking at Child #1*) You never know what's going to happen up in here.

NATE: As I was saying Prof, how 'bout some of these chicken wings?

KATESHIA: Prof? (*Sarcastically*)

NATE: (*Catching the sarcasms*) By the way Prof, this is Brenda and Ka-Tee-sha. I think she's having a bad nail day.

MANKATA:	(*Chuckles*) It is a pleasure to meet you both.
BRENDA:	Hi!
KATESHIA:	Hello. And just what do you teach, "Pro-fes-sor" Mankata? (*Aiming to correct Nate*)
MANKATA:	African Studies and International Trade.
NATE:	In case y'all hadn't noticed Prof…(*Aiming his attention to KaTeshia*) I mean "Pro-fes-sor" Mankata is from Africa – Ghana, West Africa.
KATESHIA:	(*Sarcastically*) Nawh?
BRENDA:	(*With genuine astonishmen*t) Really? How about a chicken wing Professor?
MANKATA:	(*Politely*). Perhaps a small piece. Thank you. (*Brenda gives her plate to Professor Mankata who takes a piece of chicken*)
NATE:	So what y'all think about President Clin-ton's trip to Africa?
KATESHIA:	What? (*Annoyed while others look on with interest*)
NATE:	(*Eager to inform*) President Clinton's trip to the "Motherland" a few months ago? I thought it was cool myself. That six-nation tour over there in places like South Africa, Senegal, Ghana. Man! I thought it was the bomb!

BRENDA: (*Perks up – this is a topic she knows about*) Oh! I remember that trip! It was kinda cool huh? Hanging out with President Nelson Mandela. I was really impressed when President Clinton got all decked out in traditional African wear! (*Others start to laugh at Brenda's excitement. Becoming a bit embarrassed, she continues*)

Well, I mean, like, I thought it was really cool.

REV. CLEO: (*Leans over to Deacon*)

You know what "they say."

DEACON: Nawh Rev, what "they say?"

REV. CLEO: "They say," Clinton is about as close to us evvvvv-er getting a black president as we evvvvv-er gon'get. That's what they say, Deacon.

DEACON: Yes Rev. that be right. And let me add... when a black man becomes President, you know pigs will be flying!

CHILD #1: They all so old. Ain't they heard about... (*Both children giggle*)

ALL THREE
CHILDREN: ...SWINE FLU? (*Both laugh really loud*)

CHILD #2: I don't care what "they say" I think we will have a black president one day! (*All children agree*)

NATE: (*Equally impressed by her knowledge. He now gives Brenda his full attention*) I could hang with that whole apology for "slavery thing" myself. This whole debt that America owes Black folks is long overdue, if you ask me.

BRENDA: That's interesting!

NATE: Nawh! That's a fact. But me'n Swipe really could relate to the slave castle visits since we were just in Ghana last year with Stairstep.

BRENDA: You guys were actually in Africa?

NATE: (*Feeling proud*) Yeah. You ever been?

BRENDA: No, but I went to Paris last spring with my parents. Is Africa anything like France? (*Everyone laughs*)

NATE: (*Finds the idea amusing*) I...don't think so. But, I could talk on and on about Africa for days.

KATESHIA: (*Talking softly to herself*) Yeah, I just bet you could.

NATE: Excuse me?

KATESHIA: (*Somewhat embarrassed, but still annoyed*) I said, this chicken sho' is good.

BRENDA: I want to hear about your trip.

NATE: (*Flattered over the attention*) For one thing, it made me think a lot about our Ancestors - how they were taken as captives, then brought over here to work as slaves. That's why I'm so anxious to see this Juneteenth play tonight. It sheds a little perspective on the whole situation, you know what I'm saying? (*Looks at Brenda with personal interest*)

BRENDA: (*Dreamy*) Yes, I believe I do.

KATESHIA: (*Looks at Brenda with annoyance*) I don't believe this.

SWIPE: So, Professor Mantaka, how do you see the relationship between freedom of Blacks in America to those in Africa?

KATESHIA: Well, blow me over, he really can talk!

MANKATA: Independence for most countries in Africa is more recent than you think. Ghana, for example was one of the earliest to regain its independence from the British and that was only in 1957. Actually, the struggles of Black people in the United States and Africa have been quite parallel.

KATESHIA: But, I've always thought of African people who live in Africa as being free.

MANKATA: (*All become focused on her as she speaks*) Oh, no. It was in the late 1800's that Somalia was invaded by the British. That was after slaves in the United States had been freed. Yet, Somalia did not receive her independence until 1960. Senegal and Mali gained their independence from the French only in 1960. And as you know, in South Africa, under Dutch and British invasions, laws were implemented where Blacks were forbidden to own land. Up until 1986, Blacks were barred from moving from one district to another without a "pass" or a "permission paper" in South Africa. Does this sound familiar?

KATESHIA: (*With disgust*) Yeah, American slavery perhaps.

MANKATA: As I stated before, there is much to be learned from this shared struggle of Black people.

BRENDA: Wow! That's powerful.

SWIPE: (*Speaking directly to Brenda*) The irony of it all is because Africa is a powerful and rich continent. And it's all about economics! (*Brenda nods in agreement*)

MANKATA: The Europeans wanted rights to the womb of Africa. She was often raped of her treasures for their personal profits and pleasures - the gold, her diamonds ... (*Waitress re-enters with Swipe and Nate's orders*)

NATE: …The oil, copper, cattle, animal skins...

SWIPE: …Not to mention the physical labor of African people. But the crazy thing was, many Europeans actually believed it was a privilege for Africans to be ruled by them. Ain't that nothing!

MANKATA: (*With a bit of humor*) That you will learn more about during second semester. But this play you speak of should give an interesting perspective on the emancipation of African people enslaved in this country.

KATESHIA: Just what is this play about anyhow? (*Showing interest*)

NATE: It's about Juneteenth. You do know what Juneteenth is don't you Ka-Te-shia? (*Brenda offers them wings, Nate accepts and begins eating, Swipe declines*)

KATESHIA: (*Facetiously*) Yeah! It's a time to hang out and have a good time with Black folks in the park and stuff.

SWIPE: (*Speaks directly to KaTeshia*) A lot of people think Juneteenth is about hanging out in a park, drinking red soda pop, and eating barbecue all day. But, there's more to it than that.

KATESHIA: (*Sarcastically*) So, Man of few words, why don't you just break it down to us then.

SWIPE: (*Takes on her challenge and speaks with confidence*) It's a free thang - knowledge. And it's cool, you know? (*KaTeshia looks somewhat embarrassed*)

Back in 1863 when our boy, Lincoln so-called "freed the slaves", not all of them got word of their release from captivity. Some states were in rebellion against anti-slavery laws and chose not to comply. Texas being one of 'em. So, a lot of people didn't get word about being free for over two and a half years later.

BRENDA: Really? (*Gives Nate another chicken wing*)

SWIPE: Many so called "slave owners" rebelled against "slave laws" and started migrating from the South and Eastern states over toward Texas where they knew slavery was still going on. Then they could keep people held as captives without it being a genuine crime.

KATESHIA: Then what? (*Intrigued by Swipe's knowledge*)

SWIPE: (*Starting to like the shift in her attitude*) Then, they kept buying and selling Black folks like it was nobody's business until finally in 1865, General Gordon Granger "gallantly" showed up in Texas and said, "Fun's over y'all! Let them people go and bust ya'own butts for a change." (*Swipe notices piece of kente cloth on the floor, picks it up, gestures to people asking if it's their's. No one claims it, he holds it inquisitively for a bit.*)

KATESHIA: Really? (*Looks admirably at Swipe*)

SWIPE: (*Turns attention from kente cloth, responds appreciatively to KaTeshia*) Really.

(*Places kente cloth in his pocket*)

BRENDA: So, where is this play, exactly?

NATE: At the "Great American History Theatre" in St. Paul. Y'all thinking about going?

BRENDA: I'd like to…

KATESHIA: …Perhaps. And if so, we'll meet you there. (*Returns to her apprehensive manner*)

NATE: That'll work too. It'll be a group of us there from Professor Mankata's class. So, we'll get there early enough to save you some good seats. Won't we, man?

SWIPE: True dat! True dat! (*Really chomping into his food*)

KATESHIA: Ump! Ump! Ump! He's rewound himself back onto moron mode.

BRENDA: Yeah, but look! His appetite's moved into fast-forward. (*End of scene; all exit*)

MUSIC: Instrumental "*Kumbaya*" in upbeat tempo for about 15 seconds. (*Strike restaurant scene – remove tables, chairs, counter, dishes.*)

ACT ONE

SCENE TWO

TIME: Next Evening.

PLACE: A theater in Saint Paul, Minnesota. While
                         pre-recorded Announcers voice is being
                         played, *Nate* and *Brenda* quickly exit
                         backstage then enter theater and take seats
                         in front row with the audience. *KaTeshia*
                         and *Swipe* also exit backstage quickly.
                         Their lines are delivered from rear of the-
                         ater in order for them to return expediently
                         backstage and prepare for their historical
                         characters, *Lewis* and *Florence*. All char-
                         acters remain backstage for scene change.
                         Professor Mankato, prepares for histor-
                         ical character, *Yaa Asantewaa*; *Waitress*
                         prepares for historical character, *Mama*;
                         Children #1, 2, and 3 prepare for *Sam-
                         uel*, *Alice*, *Luke*. By the time Announcer
                         finishes play introduction, *Nate* and
                         Brenda are seated in audience. Their lines
                         are delivered from the audience. When
                         finished, both exit rear of theater; return
                         backstage and prepare for their historical
                         characters *Abby* and *Leroy*.

ANNOUNCER: NOTE: (*Director/Producer information is changed to reflect applicable production.*)

(*PRE-RECORDED*) Ladies and gentlemen: Welcome to *Kumbayah ... the Juneteenth Story* - a play written by Rose McGee, originally directed by James A. Williams. Originally produced by Arts-Us and The Twin Cities Juneteenth Committee. So as not to distract the actors during performance and as a form of courtesy to others sitting in the audience, we ask that you adhere to the following: Please remain seated throughout the entire performance. Small children are welcome; however, please remove them from the theater should they become too playful or begin to cry. Taking pictures, videotaping or audio taping is prohibited. Do not use laser pointers. If you have cell phones or pagers, turn them off now!

Immediately following the play, please remain seated and partake in a 30-minute discussion regarding the performance of *Kumbayah ... The Juneteenth Story*. Thank you and please enjoy the presentation.

BRENDA: (*Seated in front row of theater with the audience; Immediately after Announcer's last line, stands up and looks towards back*) What is taking them so long to come in?

NATE: (*Stands up, begins looking around*) They must still be checking out that artwork in the lobby. Swipe really got into that sculpture of Dred Scott.

BRENDA: Oh! Here they come. Finally!

NATE: (*Yells out to them*) Hey! Swipe, KaTeshia over here! Good seats down here!

KATESHIA: (*Entering from rear of theater*) I don't believe he just did that. His elevator must have stopped on basement level at birth!

BRENDA: (*Starts to wave over the crowd*) KaTeshia! What took you so long?

KATESHIA: (*Looks at Brenda with disgust*) Shh! Girl, please. (*turns to Swipe and speaks to him*) This is so embarrassing. I hope nobody sees me that I know. I am not walking down in front of those people after that scene. Let's go sit in the balcony somewhere. (*KaTeshia and Swipe exit theater to prepare for Lewis and Florence roles.*)

BRENDA: Hey! Where are you going?

NATE: Okay then…we'll just come and sit back there with you guys! (*Brenda and Nate run down the aisle, exit out the theater and go backstage lights go down.*)

ACT ONE

SCENE THREE

CURTAINS DRAWN

TIME: Early 1863

PLACE: Turner Plantation in Grimes, Texas.

MUSIC: Instrumental upbeat tempo, "Walk In Jerusalem." Song plays for about 30 seconds.

SET: Curtains still drawn. Behind the curtain, stage being set to Turner Plantation.

NOTE: Although script is written with *Samuel, Daniel, Stuart, Luke, Alice*, roles can be changed to reflect more girls. *Samuel* can be *Samuella*, etc. More children can be in the scene, just not necessarily with speaking lines.

FREDERICK
DOUGLASS: (*Douglass enters from behind curtain to front of stage and begins speaking directly to the audience. Douglass is dressed in formal wear of the 1860s era. Character can only be seen by audience*) Well! Hear tell y'all came to hear more about Juneteenth. Is that right? (*pauses a moment*) I said is that right?

AUDIENCE: That's right!

DOUGLASS: (*Nods acknowledging audience's response*) Well then.

I, Frederick Douglass, was well known in my day for delivering eloquent speeches and "stories" such as this one. Now this story, like all stories, has a beginning and of course, a setting. The setting could take place most anywhere in the South, but, for the sake of simplicity let's just talk about a small vicinity of Texas.

I grew up knowing a great deal about this so called "slavery." After all, I was born in it around 1817. However, I could not tolerate it. So, at age 20, I escaped. My father was said to have been a white man, although I never knew him.

I never traveled much to Texas, but I certainly kept my attention fixed on conditions, thereof. It was destined for me to inform the world of human suffrage - the beatings, the lynching; selling and separating children from their parents; husbands from their wives; being forbidden to read or write or to even speak in their native African tongues. (*Projects emotion as anger builds*) Certainly, I could speak endlessly and compellingly about the horrors of captivity. (*Calms down*) But, back to the story.

You see, in 1863, Abraham Lincoln put a mechanism in place to dissolve slavery in this country. It was called the *Emancipation*? (*Pauses for audience to respond*)

AUDIENCE: *Proclamation.*

DOUGLASS: Yes, that's right! The *Emancipation Proclamation.* He even conferred with me and a few others on the wording. I strongly opposed the wording (*Pauses*), but that's another story. Of the thirty-three states, none of the "slave states" were willing to comply with his Proclamation. Eleven of them had already left the Union.

Well...there was a place over in Texas called Grimes...

(*CURTAIN RISES; REVEALS TURNER PLANTATION*)

MUSIC: (*Instrumental music starts "Walk In Jerusalem"*)

DOUGLASS: ...And over in Grimes was the Turner Plantation, which was a better place to live than most because Ole Man Turner tried to treat his Negroes with some concern for their welfare. For one thing, he didn't allow excessive brutality on his property.

(*In pantomime: The Turner Plantation cast comes on stage doing some type of chore. Director's discretion for entrances and exits. All are dressed in slave attire – old, ragged cloths. Enter Samuel, Daniel, Alice, Luke, Stuart playing together. The black children wear no shoes; the white children do wear shoes. Still in pantomime, enter Florence, Abby chatting together. Enter Rev. Cleo, Mama, and some others, busy, but keeping it moving across stage and off stage. Enter young Tellers interacting and engaged in plantation chores. Florence is carrying a basket of cloths. She drops the basket. As she and Abby begin picking up items, enter Lewis from stage right. He begins helping Florence and carries the basket for her. They appear to have a romantic interest in each other. As the two of them exit stage left, Abby and all the other children exit stage right. Samuel, Daniel, Alice, Luke, Stuart remain on stage – obviously trouble among them. All this is done while Douglass is still speaking.*)

DOUGLASS: On the Turner Plantation lived a young Black man named, Lewis. Well, in some ways he reminded me of myself when I was his age. Oh, he was a "trumpet for freedom" all right. Indeed he was. Many described Lewis as being somewhat of a "protector" for others. One day....

ALICE: (*Pouting and mad with the others*) ...Pis-ca-pay-lun's don't!

LUKE: We sure don't. Ain't never heard tell of such a thing!

SAMUEL: (*In a heavy tease on Alice*) Naw-uh, gots to be Baptist. You needs da wadda, Girl!

ALICE: Well, Med-di-dous, den. Dey jess sprinkle wadda on top of yo' head!

LUKE: Just like us I guess. Cause my Mama says we're Methodists and we just get sprinkled.

STUART: My Daddy says he don't care, long as we ain't Catholic, whatever that is.

SAMUEL: (*Looks puzzled at Stuart*) I don't know either! (*Turns to Alice pretends to dunk Daniel in the water*). But Alice you's gon' be baptized in de river!

ALICE: Naw I ain't! Dey ain't takn' me unda no wadda talkn' bout baptiz'n me.

DANIEL: Rev. Cleo says dat's de only way to wash yo' sins away! (*Imitates Rev. Cleo*)

ALICE: Den I jess stay fulla sins den, cauz I ain't go'n unda no wadda!

SAMUEL: (*Begins imitating the preacher; Luke and Stuart show expressions of concern for poor Alice*)

            Den you know where you go'n Alice? I 'mo tell you! First, you gon' be knocked in da head wid a big o' brimstone!

DANIEL: (*Imitating amen corner*) Say dat brotha!

SAMUEL: Den, da devil his-self. I saidddd da devil his-self gon' take you down to his house!

DANIEL: Dat's right! (*Stomps to the rhythm of his words*) He gon' take.. you.. to.. his.. house!

SAMUEL: And down dare in his kitchen is where he keeps da big fir-ree furnace!

DANIEL: A-men. Bro Sam! (*Lewis enters from stage left, stops and listens to the children. They don't notice his arrival*)

SAMUEL: And da devil, he be migh-dee mean. Meaner dan young Mastah Wade, ain't he Daniel?

DANIEL: Ham mercy! And uglier too!

SAMUEL: So's you bess git in dat water, gal and git yo sins washed away or else you be go'n straight to he...(*Lewis quickly interrupts Daniel*)

LEWIS: ...Boy, watch yo' mouth, you hear me! Or I'll sho yo' behind where da fiery furnace is. Y'all ought not be pickn' on Alice like dat. Now y'all gon' somewhere and stop all dis talkn' bout fire and brimstone. (*Quickly all the children run off stage*)

ALICE: (*Mumbling to herself and Lewis, she sits down*) I ain't gon' live wid no devil, cauz I's gon' be free one day to do jess as I please. And God ain't gon' care if I went down unda dat wadda or not. (*Pauses, questions with concern*) Is he Lewis?

LEWIS: (*Consoling*) Alice, I don't know if'n God will really care or not. But, you know what? Go'n in dat water ain't so bad? I did it when I was' bout yo' age. To tell you da truth, it felt real good. Uncle Isaac wuz holdn' me up on one side and Rev. Cleo had me on de other. I was well protected. But, I sho' wuz scared. Jess like you is now. But, you know what? (*Begins to change the mood to a funny, light and humorous tone*) It turned out to be fun! Shucks, when baptiz'n wuz over, I said A-men! A-men! Take me unda again! Den da real fun part come. (*Tells the story with lots of life; makes it really a big story*)

Dey all started sing'n and prayn' over me. Ain't never had dat much attention befo'. Ole Mastah Turner even give me da day off from do'n any work. Dey had a feast jess fo' me. Dey said it wuz my eternal life on earth meal. Had my favorite foods too. Uummm, makes my mouth water jess thinkn' back on dat meal. Why, dare wuz some fried chicken, sweet ro-sha-near corn, some ginger bread, and some honey beets. Ooo wee! It was some kinda day, when I got baptized.

(*Enter Wade Turner from stage left; stands in background watching*)

ALICE: (*Relaxed*) Really?

LEWIS: Yeah. And I know dey's gon' do da same thang fo' you. Cept' maybe even more cause you's so pretty and smart.

ALICE: (*Gets an idea; jumps up from seat*) I gotta go, Lewis.

LEWIS: Hey, where you rush'n off so fast?

ALICE: I gotta go find Rev. Cleo' nem so's I can see how soon dey can baptize me! (*Lewis laughs as Alice runs off stage right. Wade Turner approaches Lewis after Alice exits.*)

WADE: (*Mean-spirited, laughing tone*) Well Boy, see'ns how you got so much time to be playing around with pickaninnies, you must not have enough to keep you busy.

LEWIS: (*Hates to, but humbles down to Wade's authority*) Afternoon, Young Mastah Wade, Suh.

WADE: I hear tell my daddy's sending you off to Galveston again in the morning to sell off some more cattle for him.

LEWIS: Yes Suh, dat be right, Suh.

WADE: (*Jealousy, anger, hurt pouring out*) You really think you something, don't you boy? My daddy's always sending you instead of me, his own son, to take care of his business! Well, you jess remember boy, I'm the one who's gon' be in charge of things around here one day. We'll see who runs things then. Enjoy it while you can, cause it won't be for long. You hear me, nigga? (*Wade exits in anger*)

MUSIC: (*Heavy, dark cords play slowly during Lewis' monologue*)

LEWIS: I can't stand dis. I jess can't stand it. (*In anger, he looks towards the sky; becomes tearful*)

Lord, why in da world you put us in dis condition? We don' sinned 'ginst you so? Forgive us den! I jess wants my freedom, Lord. I jess wants to be my own self. I don't even know my own mama or where she got sold off to. No idea who my papa wuz. Hear tell he was a white man. Help me not to be mindful of dat. If dare's white blood in my veins, help me not to hate dem fo' what dey do to us. (*Lewis falls to his knees in total submission*)

I just wants my freedom. Like dem birds flyn' round up dare in de sky. Lord and only Mastah of my life, I just wants my freedom!

MUSIC: (*Shifts from dark instrumental to powerful African drumming. As Lewis drifts further into his prayer, entering from an audience aisle are Yaa Asantewaa and the two Ancestor Children. Two Ancestor Dancers appear on stage. One dances over to Lewis creating a mystical space in time. The other is carrying the Asante Stool in a proud, majestic walk, goes over and stands behind Lewis. Lewis notices the Dancers, becomes alarmed. At this time, the music fades down, but continues to play. Dancer places stool on the floor. Yaa begins speaking from the aisle. As she moves onto the stage, the two Ancestor Children follow closely. Once on stage, the Children stand one on each side of Yaa, while the Dancers are positioned one on each side of Lewis. At all times, the Ancestor Children never stop their movement – like a breeze, they continue to move lightly. The Dancers are dressed in airy African-style clothing. Yaa is dressed in an elegant white, flowing African robe, draped with a large kente stole and two African beaded necklaces. The Ancestor Children are dressed in free-flowing, airy, African wear of pastel shades. Each has an African beaded necklace around the neck similar to the one worn by Yaa Asantewaa.*)

YAA
ASANTEWAA: (*Speaking in English and Twi a language spoken by many of the Asantes*)

Oye Obaakofoo a ye a yie wo. (*repeat three times*)

Lewis, my Son. You are one of the chosen ones. A special warrior. Your desire to be free will come soon - it is your destiny. Perhaps not according to the ways of the world, but a freedom promised to last through eternity.

ANCESTOR
CHILD #1: Others on earth will grow stronger and become more faithful because of your unselfish spirit.

ANCESTOR
CHILD #2: Others will be forced to change their evil ways because of the sacrifice of your pure heart.

LEWIS: (*Without realizing it himself, Lewis begins to speak in perfect English and utters some phrases in Twi- his own native language long forgotten*) Oye Obaakofoo a ye a yie wo. I am not drunk – for I have had no whiskey. I am not weak for I have done no plowing today. Surely, I have been robbed of sound mind.

YAA
ASANTEWAA: My Son, you are of sound mind. Do not be fearful. There is an honorable journey you are destined to take… that sacrifice.

ANCESTOR
CHILD #1: The time draws near when you must take leave of this earth. When that hour comes, do not fear. We have already been assigned to be your guides.

YAA
ASANTEWAA: Emmere Bi Be Duru Ho Aa Wo Be Tu Wo Kwan Saa Emmere No Duru Ho Aa Nsuro Efirese Yankopon Yeyem Se Ye Me Hwee Wo So.

LEWIS: Where do you come from? And what do you speak of – sacrifice?

YAA
ASANTEWAA: You are full of vision, Lewis. I represent the compassion of your own mother, the privilege of your natural father and the wisdom of your own being. (*Ancestor Children guide Yaa to Asante Stool to be seated*)

ANCESTOR
CHILD #2: (*As story is being told, Yaa sits on the Asante Stool as though in a trance*) She comes in the form of Yaa Asantewaa, Queen Mother of the Asante Empire.

ANCESTOR
CHILD #1:   Her life will not end as quickly as yours.
                         But hers will also be a sacrifice. Her des-
                         tiny is to "protect" the Golden Stool. The
                         stool is believed to contain the soul of her
                         people and will hold them in unity.

ANCESTOR
CHILD #2:   She will be placed in exile by the British
                         for courageously leading her Asante army
                         into the most bloodiest of Anglo-Asante
                         wars.

ANCESTOR
CHILD #1:   She will be sentenced to die in 1923. Her
                         legacy will be left as an example of brav-
                         ery for centuries to come Lewis, just as
                         yours will be.

ANCESTOR
CHILD #2:   All of what is happening at this moment,
                         you will not remember.

ANCESTOR
CHILD #1:   You will not remember.

ANCESTOR
CHILD #2:   You will not remember.

YAA
ASANTEWAA: Now, go in comfort, knowing that God and the Ancestors are with you. (*Yaa places two of the three necklaces she is wearing around Lewis' neck*)

Ko Asundwemu Meba Menim Se Oyankopon Ne Nananom Nasmanfo…Ka Wo Ho. Now go in comfort, my Son knowing that God and the Ancestors are with you.

(*Yaa Asantewaa rapidly exits stage, heads down the aisle, exits theater with Ancestor Children following closely behind. Drumming becomes powerful and rapid as they exit.. Ancestor Dancers exit stage after Yaa and Children are out of theater. When Ancestor Dancers exit stage, only Lewis is left on the stage. He takes on a look of realization of having just come face to face with his own destiny. Drumming picks up. He runs off stage, exits theater down same aisle as Yaa and the children. Music plays for about 30 seconds, then transitions into next scene.*)

Act One

Scene Four

TIME: Later Same Day.

PLACE: Turner Plantation.

MUSIC: Instrumentals, upbeat temp. *Florence, Samuel, Stuart, Luke* are together. She's busy digging around in *Samuel's* head for hidden cuckaberries (*Small dried up thistles with sticky points that attach themselves to whatever they touch*). *Luke* and *Stuart* look on in awe. *Lewis* enters. He has no-recollection of his mystical encounter. Remaining out of their view for a while, he observes the humor of their exchange before making his presence known. Music stops. Dialogue begins.

SAMUEL: Ouch!

FLORENCE: Boy, sit still if you want me to pick all these cuckaberries outta your head. Cause if Mama sees them you'll be in a mighty heap of trouble.

SAMUEL: Ouch! You aint got to be so rough, Floey.

FLORENCE: It's your own fault for playing 'round in that patch of thickets anyhow. You not suppose to be down there. You know better. (*Looks at Stuart, Luke*) And you two ain't no better. Ought to be ashamed of yo' selves! The three of you put together ain't got the sense of a...

SAMUEL: ...Ouch!

FLORENCE: Hold still!

SAMUEL: How come Mastah Luke and Mastah Stuart don't never git no cuckaberries caught up in dey heads?

LUKE: (*Puzzled*) Yeah, Floey, how come?

FLORENCE: (*Not wanting to get into hair texture, she stops and looks at all three of them; shakes her head in frustration*)

Maybe cauz there ain't enough to go around by the time Sam gets all of 'em stuck up in his head. Mastah Stuart, you're the oldest – you should set the example. Now keep away from that swamp.

STUART: Wasn't my fault Floey. It wuz Sam's idea. All Sam's!

LUKE: Wasn't all Sam's fault Floey. We wanted to go down there too.

FLORENCE: Giant rattle snakes hide out down there near that swamp. And they just waitn' for little boys like you to fill up their stomachs with.

STUART: I bet you my daddy ain't afraid of no rattlers. My daddy says he can shoot anything faster'n anybody 'round these parts (*Stands up and acts like he's aiming a rifle*) …and that's how come he aint't never had no runaway slaves.

LUKE: (*Gets agitated*) Hush up, Stuart! No sense in talkn' bout nobody running away.

FLORENCE: That's enough talk about shooting and runaways, Mastah Stuart.

SAMUEL: (*Bragging*) I ain't scared of no rattlers. I don't care how big they is. Ouch! (*Lewis approaches and moves past Florence closer to Samuel*)

LUKE: Sam ain't feared of nothing, are you Sam?

STUART: He's scared of my daddy, ain't you Sam? Everybody scared of my daddy.

LUKE: My daddy says yo' daddy's just (*Makes a big puff and blows out*) fulla air, Stuart.

STUART: Is not!

LUKE: Is so!

FLORENCE: Boys, stop it…right now!

SAMUEL: Ah, let'em fuss, Floey. Dey do it all da time. (*Gets feisty with Floey*) And hurry up and git through wid my head! (*Lewis steps in and startles them all*)

LEWIS: Boy! Don't sassy yo'sistah! She's tell'n you right. And stay way from down dare near dat swamp... (*Lewis pulls Samuel's hair*)

SAMUEL: Ouch, Lewis.

FLORENCE: (S*urprised over Lewis' arrival, immediately begins to groom her hair, checks her clothes to make sure she's presentable.*) Why Lewis, you scared me half to death. I didn't even hear you come up.

SAMUEL: Dat's cauz he always mov'n round real quiet like a haint or somethn'.

LEWIS: Like a haint, do I? Dat's so's I can keep my ghostly eyes on yo' mischief. Boo! (*Samuel jumps, then begins to laugh. Florence laughs. Lewis turns his attention to the boys*) Gottcha again!

           (*Lewis begins telling the story with lots of animation and drama*)

One a' Ole Misses' cats wandered off into dem thickets and got swallowed up whole by a big ole rattla dats been living near dat swamp for ages. And last year, same thang happen' to one of ole Mastah's hound dogs. (*Lewis picks Luke up and swings him in the air as he tells the story. Luke's eyes are filled with fun and anticipation. The others are all in awe and listen deeply to the story*)

Dey say dat every now and den – don't matter if'n it be day or night dat ole rattla come creepn' outta dat swamp area jess lookn' fo' somethn' live to gulp up and swolla down – BOO!

(*They all jump; he places Luke back on the ground. Lewis laughs with them for a moment then turns to Samuel*) Is dis yo' day for meddl'n round or what? (*Pulls Samuel's hair again*)

SAMUEL: Ouch Lewis!

FLORENCE: (*Lets out a squeal*)

LEWIS: (*Turns his attention to Florence*) Florence, I'm sorry if'n I scared you.

FLORENCE: (*Blushing*) Oh, that's all right Lewis.

SAMUEL: (*Imitating the blushing Florence*) "Oh dat's all right, Lewis."

(*Begins to chant*)

Florence is sweet on Lew-is, Florence is sweet on Lew-is.

FLORENCE: (*Embarassed*) Hush yo' mouth, Samuel. As a matter of fact, you best get along and do your chores before I tell Mama all about what you been doing today.

LEWIS: Yeah, like tryn' to scare po' little Alice half to death 'bout go'n to da devil and a fiery furnace.

FLORENCE: I didn't know you been so busy today, Samuel. I think Mama ought'a know what you been up to.

SAMUEL: (*Senses the need to get away from potential punishment*)

Nawh, don't tell Mama!

LUKE: (*Recognizes that his friend needs a deterrent*) Sam, wanna come help us feed the pigs?

SAMUEL: (*Feeling rescued*) I can't think of nothn' I wanna do better right now. Gotta go see after da pigs now, Floey. Bye, Lewis. Nice to see ya.

LEWIS: (*Stops Samuel dead in his tracks*) Hold on a minute. You stay outta trouble, ya hear me? And mind what yo' sistah be tell'n ya.

SAMUEL: All right, I will! (*Runs off stage with Stuart and Luke*)

FLORENCE: (*Recognizing that they are alone. Lewis seizes chance to share his dreams and his intentions with Florence. She appears shy and uncertain of what to do with the moment and picks a safe topic – the weather*)

It sho is a pretty day today.

LEWIS: (*Lewis recognizes that Florence is shy, but decides to take a chance anyway. To him, she is the prettiest girl in the world – so he picks what comes naturally to him – the truth*)

Not as pretty as you is. I don't think nuthn' is pretty as you is Florence.

FLORENCE: (*Florence sees Lewis as being handsome, smart and worldly*) Oh, I bet you be telling a lotta girls the same thing off in them places you be traveling for Ole Mastah Turner.

LEWIS: (*With deep sincerity*) Nawh. (*pauses*) Jess you. Ah… Florence? I bought you a little somethn'. Got this when I was in Tyler last week. I hope you like it. (*Hands her a pretty piece of ribbon*)

FLORENCE: Why this is beautiful. You always giving me such nice things, Lewis.

LEWIS: You deserve nice thangs. When I gets free I hope to take you…well…dare's a lot of nice places I want you to see with me one day, Florence. I…

FLORENCE: (*Stopping him which changes the mood somewhat*) Lewis, you always talkn' 'bout freedom. Do you think we ever gon' get our freedom?

LEWIS: Of course, I do. And I knows it's gon' be soon. You gotta believe dat Florence. Can you keep a secret? Mastah Turner don' promised me dat when I turns 21, I can have my freedom. Den he gon' hire me for my services. Next month I be turn'n 21, Florence. I be earn'n wages. I's gon' be as free as a bird. (*Becomes very animated*) And dat's just what I's gon' feel like do'n too…fly like a bird. A big o' eagle as a matter of fact! Look up dare, Florence. (*He points upward*) See dat tall cliff, I go up dare a lot to just sit and thank 'bout thangs. I look over da valley sometimes and sees da people workn' hard with da sun beatn' down on 'em and I wonders to myself, how come dis happen to us? Some of us is from kings and queens. We had our own villages, raised our own crops and animals. We wuz free in Africa. It ain't right dat white folks come over to our home and took us and made us dey property.

FLORENCE: (*Speaks solemnly*) No, Lewis, it ain't right.

LEWIS: Dat's how come, I know it won't be long fo' we's all gon' be free. But, I'm gon' be free next week. And den, I'm com'n to take you fo' my wife and make you free. (*Lewis startled himself and Florence with his words*)

I's sorry, Florence...I mean if'n you will have me. I mean. I guess I ain't sayn' dis right (*Gets down on his knees, takes her hand*)

Florence, would you mind jumpn' da broom wid me and com'n my wife?

FLORENCE: (*She's surprised and ecstatic*) Oh, Lewis, do you mean it? (*He nods - fearful that she may say, no*) Yes! Oh, yes, Lewis. (*Wade appears on stage; observes the two; becomes filled with jealousy; neither of them sees Wade*)

LEWIS: (*Almost speechless from delight*) Oh, thank you, Florence. Thank you for say'n, "Yes." I will always protect you, Florence. Even when I ain't wid you. I feel somehow I should be tak'n care of you. I always want to do dat and dat's a promise. I ain't got no mama and papa to fuss over. So I's jess as soon fuss over you and Sam and yo' mama too, cauz I's plans on buying all'a y'all's freedom too. (*Pauses, then speaks most passionately*) I loves you, Florence.

FLORENCE: I love you too, Lewis. (*He leans over and kisses her gently on the cheek. Neither knows what to say next that's appropriate, so Lewis makes the next move*)

LEWIS: I's got to leave in the morn'n fo' to take some cows to Galveston. But when I returns, next month, I returns a free man, Florence. (*Remembers the necklaces*). Oh and dare's one other thang I wanna give you. (*He removes one of the beaded necklaces and places it around her neck*)

LEWIS: Now we both have one for "protection."

FLORENCE: Lewis, this is wonderful. It feels so warm like a beating heart around my neck or something.

LEWIS: Dat's cause our hearts beat as one, Florence.

FLORENCE: Oh and before I forget. I made you something (*She pulls out a beautiful piece of kente fabric which is same pattern seen in restaurant that Swipe found on the floor*). Happy birthday, Lewis. This hankie is from a piece of cloth that my grand-mama wore – my daddy's mama. It's all she had on when they sold her off to some people a long ways from here. My daddy gave it to my mama. She gave it to me when I got old enough to ask questions about it. My Mama seems to think the spirit of Africa and our Ancestors live in each piece of thread. (*She shows him the patterns. Together they examine the cloth*) I wanted you to have a piece of it with you always. Turning 21 is a mighty special occasion. And you might need guidance from the Ancestors. (*Shyly*) ...and it might help you to think of me.

LEWIS: Thank you, Florence. Dis be mighty special. It's beautiful jess like you. And it's soft to hold jess like you. (*To avoid disrespecting Florence in any way, he reaches and holds her hand. Slowly he releases it*) It's git'n' late. Guess I better git go'n. Thank about me. I'll be thankn' on you everyday...and night.

FLORENCE: I will think on you, Lewis, day and night. (*She reaches for the beads around her neck*) I will. (*Excited and in love, he runs down the aisle out of theater; Florence sings solo*)

SONG:

"Love Will Find A Way" ©
By Ben Emboya Ward

I know you're not far away, but I won't be afraid.
I know our love is here to stay.
And just like a road that spans across the sea,
love will be a bridge for you and me.
I know...love will be a bridge for you and me.
I know you're not far away, but I won't be afraid.
I know our love is here to stay.
And just like a road, that spans across the sea,
love will be a bridge for you and me.
I know...love will be a bridge for you and me.
I know...love will be a bridge for you and me.

(*Wade approaches her after song is completed.*)

MUSIC:

Instruments shift to rattling, aggravating sounds.

WADE:

Well, well, now. If that ain't something, our little Floey talkn' bout marrying herself off. Now, my sister won't be too happy to hear that her little black play doll gon' up and get married.

FLORENCE: Mastah Wade! You been eavesdropping again?

WADE: Eavesdropping? Floey, you done had too many privileges 'round here, Gal. I own you! You ain't got no private business. My sister done raised you like you're white. You're too sassy for your own good. She done taught you how to read and write. (*Florence looks surprised*)

Did you think I didn't know what you two were up to all them times y'all was out playing schoolhouse and making mud-pies. She was teaching you how to read and write! I know how you put on that slave-talk when white folks around. But you can't fool me, Floey. You's a nigga. Always wuz and always will be. (*Moves in closer to Florence and grabs her by both arms*)

FLORENCE: Mastah Wade! What's come over you? Let me go! (*Pushes him away from her*)

WADE: (*Becomes even more agitated*) You can jess forget about marrying anybody so longs I got anything to say 'bout it. You belong to me to do as I please. And I think I'm ready to start pleasing right now. (*They begin to struggle. Wade touches Florence's neck, his hand rubs against the beaded neck-lace. The powerful heat of the beads burn his hand. He draws back quickly.*)

Ouch! (*Shocked and embarrassed, he retreats*) Ha! Ha! Ever since we were kids, you always been feisty, Floey. But, you gon' learn not to fight me. (*As reaches to grab her again, Angus calls him from back stage before he makes visible entrance*)

ANGUS: Wade! You out here, Boy? (*Florence jerks away from Wade and runs off stage, same aisle that exits theater; enter Angus*)

Oh, there you are. Thought maybe you wanna go into town with me for awhile. Something important's come up. (*Wade turns his attention toward the exit Florence made; Angus senses reason for his friend's distraction*)

Pardon me. Did I interrupt something? What's wrong with you boy? You look like some kinda luv-sick puppy. Boy, if I didn't know better, I'd swear you had a thing for that gal. (*Laughs*)

WADE: (*In anger, one step from hitting Angus*) Best you shut up Angus! I ain't got nothing for nobody.

ANGUS: Coulda fooled me. You know yo' daddy's got rules around here. Ain't no white man suppose to touch any of his coloreds. Ha! Ha! Can't even beat'm. Ha! Ha! You know everybody 'round here thinking yo' daddy's always been a little touched in the head.

WADE: Things will be different around here when I'm in charge. (*Glances in direction where Florence exited, rubs his hands, the burn from the necklace*)

         Yes, sir, mighty different.

ANGUS: From what I hear that might be real soon. Yo' daddy purt'near dead ain't he?

WADE: I don't wanna talk about that right now.

ANGUS: Well, you better talk about it. Word is he might be leaving his nigga boy, Lewis in charge of mosta all his business affairs. That sure would be a sight. Pickn' a slave to run things right over his own son. Of course he seems to already be doing that.

WADE: (*In anger, Wade grabs Angus by the collar*) You best shut up Angus and I mean right now!

ANGUS: (*Recognizes the need to back off*)

All right. Need not get so touchy about it. There's something else you might wanna know if you ain't heard about it already?

WADE: What?

ANGUS: Word done come from up North that ole Abe Lincoln serious about freeing all the coloreds. Can you beat that?

WADE: What you saying, Angus?

ANGUS: Heard my daddy and some of the others talking this morning. That Yankee's signing some kind of paper right now making it unlawful for white folks to own coloreds. Get this…He aims on settn'em free!

WADE: (*Becoming anxious*) Who else around here knows about this?

ANGUS: I don't rightly know, but my daddy and a few others are having a meeting in town this afternoon at 4:00 o'clock. That's how come I came to get you. Figured you'd wanna go into town and see what's going on.

WADE: (*With a plan running through his mind, he lowers his voice*) The fewer folks who know about this the better. Ain't no law against what people don't know. My daddy sho' don't need to hear about this. He's too sick to handle these matters And nobody else around here needs to know either.

ANGUS: (*He whispers to Wade*) What about your mama and sister?

WADE: Women folks are too delicate to be studying on such affairs. The men folks like your daddy and a few others need to hear about my idea.

ANGUS: (*Comes out of the whisper*) Well, maybe you ain't as dumb as some folks claim you are, Wade. I think that's a right smart idea. (*Begins to whisper again*) Keeping it a secret about what Abe Lincoln's doing. This is Texas and we can do what we want to over here. Come on let's get to town quick. We need to make that meeting. (*Both exit hurriedly down opposite aisle; not same as previous characters*)

ACT ONE

SCENE FIVE

TIME: Early evening, same day.

PLACE: Turner Plantation.

MUSIC: Upbeat tempo.

REV. CLEO: (*Off stage, Rev. Cleo calls the children*)

               Com'on chillum. Gon' teach y'all de Ham-
               bone! (*Running in from several directions,
               Children get on stage and sit in a circle
               around Rev. Cleo.*)

               All right now…dis is how it go. (*He does
               the hand-slaps as he sings*)

Hambone, Hambone, where you been?
'Round da world and going again.
Hambone, Hambone, have you heard?
Papa's gon' by me a mockn' bird.
If dat mockn' bird don't sing
Papa's gon' buy me a diamond ring.
Hambone, Hambone where's yo' wife?
In da kitchen cookn' rice
Now Hambone...
Now Hambone...

(*Children begin imitating him; Florence enters looking sad - still disturbed over incident with Wade. Samuel is the first to see her*)

SAMUEL: Come on Floey, play a game wid us. (*Florence does not respond. Mama enters stage carrying a basket of washing cloths. Florence goes over sits to the side to try and be alone; Other children chime in*)

ALICE: Teach us some readn' den (*Still Florence does not respond*)

DANIEL: Tell us a story den, Floey.

MAMA: (*Mama detects something is terribly wrong and intercedes*) Chillun, y'all gon' find Abby to play with y'all. Floey don't feel too well. Gon' now, git! (*Rev. Cleo senses something is wrong; feels best to exit with the children. Florence turns to Mama who already has outstretched arms. Florence falls into her arms and cries silently. Embracing and rocking Florence, Mama speaks with frustration, pain, anger*)

Come by here, Lord. When is you gon' come by here? Ain't nut'en fair 'bout bein' in slavery. People's jess property Nut'en mo'n animals. We don't own a thang. Not eben our chillum. Not eben our own bodies. Sometimes dey sees to it dat eben de innocence of bein' a child don't last fo'long. 'Specially de innocence of a young girl. But, we jess keep prayn' and holdn' on. We just keep prayn' and holdn' on.

SONG: (*Solemnly,   Florence   begins   singing
             "Kumbaya" a cappella.*)

Kumbaya, my Lord, Kumbaya
Kumbaya, my Lord, Kumbaya
Kumbaya, my Lord, Kumbaya
Oh, Lord, Kumbaya
Somebody   needs   you   Lord,
Kumbaya
Somebody   needs   you   Lord,
Kumbaya
Somebody   needs   you   Lord,
Kumbaya
Oh, Lord, Kumbaya

(*Both women begin humming as
they exit stage slowly; Once off
stage Florence finishes up the
song*)

Oh, Lord Kumbaya.

(*Strike set; prepare for Lincoln's Servants
Scene*)

ACT ONE

SCENE SIX

TIME: September 1862.

PLACE: President Abraham Lincoln's study in Washington D.C.

           (*Desk with tea pot, cups, papers scattered on top of desk and on floor. Leroy, the younger male servant is asleep in a chair – snoring with feet propped up in second chair.*)

MUSIC: Tension snare drumming.

UNCLE EARL: (*From off-stage Uncle Earl calls looking for Leroy*)

Leroy! (*Uncle Earl enters room, sees Leroy sleeping*).

Gru-umm-mmm! (*Leroy doesn't wake up. Uncle Earl grunts louder*) Gru-umm-mmm!

(*Startled, Leroy wakes up*)

Ohhhhhhhh my aching back. My knees. Oh Lord!

LEROY: Afternoon Uncle Earl. I see you walkn' mighty gen'ly taday...as usual. (*Leroy knows Uncle Earl's often fake ailments*)

Yo' ar-da-ri-dus be act'n up again? Ha! Haaaaa!

UNCLE EARL: Jess you keep on pok'n fun at Ole Earl. If'en you be smart enough to live half as long as dis ole man...which I doubt you be dat smart...you's gon' be walkn' might gen'ly too.

LEROY: Ummm hmmm. Well, it took YOU Suh, three days last week jess to polish de silverware. I can do dat in two hours...wid my eyes closed. You jess git'n old...you jess git'n old...git'n old. Ha! Ha!

UNCLE EARL: I don't know who's you thinks you is. You ain't gon' be young all yo' days, jess wait and see. Now git on wid de business of cleaning up dis here mess dat President Lincoln done made up in dis here room. Now git on! Git! Git on! (*As Leroy begins to clean, Uncle Earl quickly sits in the two chairs Leroy previously occupied*)

LEROY: Ooooooooowww wee! Look at all des papers he done just tossed all over da place. What in da world?

UNCLE EARL: (*Making himself cozy in the chairs, preparing to relax*) Yeah. I heard him up every night dis week working on some kinda speech again. And just a talkn' to hisself. Sound like he be talkn' to twenty folks.

LEROY: Is dat right? (*Begins looking at the papers closer*)

UNCLE EARL: Woun't nobody up in here but him. Po man (*Makes the loco sign with his hand towards his head*) Hmmp...hmmmp... hmmmp.

LEROY: Sho'nuff musta been writn' somethan' mighty important den.

UNCLE EARL: Musta been. (*Leaning in for a nap*)

LEROY: (*Makes a discovery on the papers; begins yelling with excitement*)

Uncle Earl! Uncle Earl!

UNCLE EARL: (*Startled from what was about to become a nap*)

Quit yelling in my ears young'un. I's aching from ar-da-ri-dus …I ain't gon deaf!

LEROY: Uncle Earl, President Lincoln done write somethn' mighty important dis time!

UNCLE EARL: Is you done lost yo'mind yo own self? Jess cauz you done learnt how to read, don't be readn' President Lincoln's papers! Now put dat down and git back to de business of clean'n up dis here mess. Gon' now git!

LEROY: Listen! Listen! Listen!

UNCLE EARL: Git to work!

LEROY: It's all wrote down right here, "I Abraham Lincoln, President of de United States and Commander-in Chief of de Army and Navy thereof…"

UNCLE EARL: …I knows he be de President and Commander-in-Chief…I knows dis already.

LEROY: Listen! Listen! Listen! "Do hereby proclaim and declare dat it is my purpose upon de next meetn' of Congress to again recommend da immediate or gradual a..a.. abo-li-tion of slavery."

UNCLE EARL: (*Sudden interest*) What dat mean – immediate or gradual abo-lition of slavery? What dat mean?

LEROY:	(*Becomes very serious*) I believe he aims on setn' black folks free...and pro'bly kinda soon.
UNCLE EARL:	(*Extremely interested*) Oh Lord! What else he don write on dat paper?
LEROY:	I thought you didn't want me to be readn'.
UNCLE EARL:	I's yo Elder, what else he done write?
LEROY:	"It is my purpose upon da next meetn' of Congress" (*Pauses and looks at Uncle Earl*) Shouldn' be too far from now. (*Continues to read*). "To Again recommend da immediate or gradual abolition of slavery of dos states in rebellion against de Union. On de first day of January in de year of our Lord one thousand and eight hundred" (*Pauses in amazement*). "One thousand eight-hundred and sixty-three!"
UNCLE EARL:	(*Astonished*) Dat be about right now alright.
LEROY:	Dat's next year! "All persons held as slaves within any State, or any de-sig-nated part of a State, da people whereof, shall den be in rebellion against de United States, shall be, henceforth and forever..." (*Pauses*)
UNCLE EARL:	What it say? What it say?
LEROY:	"Free."

UNCLE EARL: Free? Did you say free? Did you say free?

LEROY: Dat's what it says right here. He aim'n to set Black folks free.

UNCLE EARL: No wonder he been so upset. Dat man done lost his mind fo'sho!

LEROY: I don't know if'n he done lost his mind, but I sho is happy!

UNCLE EARL: Dis here calls for a celebration. (*Begins singing and dancing*) She be com'n round da mountain when she come. She be com'n round da mountain when she come. OOOOOOOHHHH! My Back! (*Leroy rushes to the older man's aid, knowing he's not faking this time*)

LEROY: Uncle Earl, yo' ar-da-ri-das?

UNCLE EARL: Oh, I's be alright! I's be alright!

LEROY: Sit down Uncle Earl and take it easy. Shall I pour you a cup of tea, Suh?

UNCLE EARL: Why yes... Soon-to-be-Free-Suh. And please do sit down and join Soon- to-be-Free-Me.

LEROY: Yes, Suh, I b'lieve I will. (*Both now holding tea cups*)

UNCLE EARL: A toast to freedom! (*Both actors freeze; enter Douglass*)

DOUGLASS: (*Looks upon the two Servants with joy, then speaks to audience*)

"My Brothers and Sisters, there's nothing greater than to honor and cherish the memory of a great public man long after he's passed onto the shadows to the silent continent of eternity."

I'm afraid I must tell you that in the fullest sense of the word, Abraham Lincoln was not "our" man nor was he "our" model. In so far as Black people were concerned, the leaders of the so-called Republic Party as it was, have always done wrong from choice, but right from necessity. However, in Lincoln's case, at least he did something.

This matter weighed heavily on his mind. He said to me once: "The fiery trials through which we pass shall light us down in honor or dishonor to the latest generation." Hmm...that would include those of you sitting in the audience and your children and their children who must be taught an accurate account of their history. (*Begins to speak with greater intensity – to the point of sounding angry*).

They must establish a burning desire to learn and soak up all the knowledge their thirsty minds can hold. They must become educated! THEY MUST BECOME EDUCATED!

MUSIC: (*Volume rises and plays for about 15 seconds.*)

BLACKOUT.

END OF ACT ONE

ACT ONE

SCENE SIX B

OPTIONAL:	If used at all, this Scene can be used in place of the previous scene or it can be used before the previous scene if you want to have a longer show.
TIME:	September 1862.
PLACE:	President Abraham Lincoln's study in Washington D.C.
MUSIC:	Tension snare drumming.
	(*Lincoln is sitting at his desk pondering over whether or not to sign his Emancipation Proclamation. Inner-conscious creates the sound of angry voices ringing in his head. From behind stage, several adult-sounding actors are assigned the following Voices.*)
VOICE:	Sign it!
VOICE:	End slavery! Stop the war!

VOICE: Let the oppressed go free. God will surely judge us all if you don't.

VOICE: There's the Union to think about.

VOICE: Do the States run the Union or does the Union run the States?

VOICE: Do not sign it!

VOICE: Even Britain has wiped its hands of slave trade.

VOICE: Free labor in the South means us Northerners work twice as hard.

VOICE: It's morally wrong to hold humans in bondage.

VOICE: World Trade will shut off from us if we don't rid slavery in this country.

VOICE: Give them "gradual" emancipation. (*Enter Lincoln's wife, Mary Todd Lincoln, carrying a tea server – tray, pot, cup. She is unable to hear the voices he hears.*)

VOICE: Sign it!

VOICE: Sign it!

MARY TODD
LINCOLN: (*Senses he's deeply troubled*)

Are you alright Dear? I brought you some tea. (*He slowly moves his head up and down. She studies his face for a moment*)

I think you should do whatever needs to be done to rid the Country of this hateful war. (*He looks up at her for a brief moment with a painful glare, then back down to his papers*). What have you written?

ABRAHAM
LINCOLN: (*With mixed emotions, he looks at her again; begins to read*)

"I, Abraham Lincoln, President of the United States, and Commander-in-Chief of the Army and Navy thereof, do hereby proclaim and declare that it is my purpose upon the next meeting of Congress to again recommend... the immediate or gradual abolition of slavery."

(*He stops reading, looks at her.*)

MARY TODD
LINCOLN: I fully understand. (*She takes the time to pour him a cup of tea in silence before speaking*) You have my support. (*She lays a gentle hand on his shoulder, leaves the tray and exits*)

ABRAHAM
LINCOLN: (*Alone, he reads aloud*)

"It is my purpose upon the next meeting of Congress to again recommend the immediate or gradual abolition of slavery of those states in rebellion against the Union. On the first day of January in the year of our Lord one thousand eight hundred and sixty three, all persons held as slaves within any State, or any designated part of a State, the people whereof, shall then be in rebellion against the United States, shall be then, henceforth and forever free."

(*Struggling to sign the papers, his hands begin shaking uncontrollably. The voices start up again – chanting together*)

VOICES: Sign it! Sign it! Sign it! Sign it! Sign it!

ABRAHAM
LINCOLN: (*Signs the paper. Then lets out a loud scream, then freezes; Douglass enters, stands looking upon Lincoln and begins monologue*)

NOTE: If both scenes are used. Stop here for end of Act One. If only this scene is used and not the Servants, continue to the end of this scene.

MUSIC: (*Instrumental, "Battle Hymn of Republic," upbeat tempo. Music is played under Douglass' monologue.*)

DOUGLASS: (*Looks upon Lincoln for a while speaks to audience*)

"My Brothers and Sisters, there's nothing greater than to honor and cherish the memory of a great public man long after he's passed onto the shadows to the silent continent of eternity."

I'm afraid I must tell you that in the fullest sense of the word, Abraham Lincoln was not "our" man nor was he "our" model. In so far as Black people were concerned, the leaders of the so-called Republic Party as it was, had always done wrong from choice, but right from necessity. However, in Lincoln's case, at least he did something.

This matter weighed heavily on his mind. He said to me once: "The fiery trials through which we pass shall light us down in honor or dishonor to the latest generation."

Hmm…that would include those of you sitting in the audience and your children and their children who must be taught an accurate account of their history. (*Begins to speak with greater intensity – to the point of sounding angry*).

They must establish a burning desire to learn and soak up all the knowledge their thirsty minds can hold. They must become educated! THEY MUST BECOME EDUCATED!

(*Douglass exits the stage in haste down same aisle used by Yaa Asantewaa.*)

MUSIC: (*Volume rises and plays for about 15 seconds after Lincoln and Douglass exits*)

BLACKOUT.

END OF ACT ONE

ACT TWO

Act Two

Scene One

TIME: January 1863

PLACE: The Turner Plantation.

(*Using several points of entrance, Florence, Abby, and the children enter theater. Florence begins a West African call and response chant. Once on stage, they all sit in circle around Florence as she sits on the tree stomp teaching them to read in secret.*)

FLORENCE:	Ja-li-a a-la-le Kaa
CHILDREN:	Ja-li-a a-la-le Kaa
FLORENCE:	Ja-li-a da-i
CHILDREN:	Ja-li-a da-i
FLORENCE:	Ja-li-a a-la-le Kaa
CHILDREN:	Ja-li-a a-la-le Kaa
FLORENCE:	Ja-li-a da-i
CHILDREN:	Ja-li-a da-i

FLORENCE: Now look at this line and repeat after me, "For God so loved the world…"

CHILDREN: (*In unison*) "For God so loved the world..."

FLORENCE: "That he gave..."

CHILDREN: (*In unison*) "That He gave..."

SAMUEL: "Dat He gave..."

FLORENCE: (*Turns to Samuel*) No, not "dat."Try and say "that."

SAMUEL: It's hard for me to say, "dat" like you do, Floey.

FLORENCE: It just takes practice. Look at how it's written, see?

MAMA: (*Enter Mama. She sees the scene becomes very upset*) Floey! Girl, you know better dan to be teachn' dem chillun to read. And in broad day light. Abby, you ole 'nuff to know better. Gon' now and take dese chillums off somewhere else to play.

ABBY: But, if we can sing all day long fo' ole Mastah, seems like we oughta be able to read and write.

MAMA: Abby! Girl, whut's com' over you? You git'n worse dan Floey.

ABBY: Well, it's da truth. Dey always want us to come sing and dance at da big parties – even when it be mighty hot. So I jess can't see how come we can't read and write to.

MAMA: Cause we ain't free, dat's how come. Now, don't sassy me no furtha. Gon's take dem chillum on outta here.

                (*Addressing Florence*) Girl, Ole Mastah will break his word and whip you fo' sure if'n he finds out. Eben worse, he might sell you off, Floey. And I couldn't bear dat.

FLORENCE: Mama, don't fret so much. Ole Mastah won't do no such thing. Besides, I believe he already knows, Mama. Nobody's gon' separate the rest of us. We all gon' be free, someday. (*For a brief moment she believes*)

MAMA: (*Begins to reflect*).One day. Maybe we will. Maybe we will. You wuz jess a little thang and I still was carrn' Samuel in my belly when Ole Mastah's evil brother came here and told us he don' lost yo' papa to slick white man gambln' on a river boat a long ways from here – a place called New O'leens. Den dey went to dat man's home to a place called Englun somewhere. Ole Mastah wuz so mad he almost kilt his own brother. Say dey had no choice, but to pay up on account of honor and everythang. He never allowed his brother to set foot on his land again. But dat didn't bring my Joseph back. Oh, honey, don't you see. I don't ever wanna to lose you and Samuel like dat.

FLORENCE: Don't worry, Mama, you won't. (*Changes the subject so her Mama will feel better*) Mama, tell me again what papa looked like. I always want to keep him written in my mind.

MAMA: (*Smiling girlishly*) Well, yo' Papa was a mighty fine lookn' man fo' one thang. And he was also very gentle and lovn'. Kinda put me in the mind young Lewis.

FLORENCE: Ah, Mama! (*Shyly*)

MAMA: I see da way you two be lookn' at each other when y'all thank nobody lookn'. Dat Lewis be a fine young man, Floey.

FLORENCE: What about Papa, Mama? Finish telling me the story.

MAMA: Anyway, I can still see my Joseph's face just as clear in my mind. He had pearly white teeth. Dem African teeth I use to tell him. Dem purty white African teeth. Course his arms was strong. He had muscles as hard as cannon balls. And he was tall, very tall.

FLORENCE: How did you know that you was in love with him?

MAMA: Oh, I know'd da first time I ever saw him. He said I 'minded him of Africa. (*Smiling from the memory*)

I was sold here when I was 15 years-old from da Pruitt Plantation. Yo' papa was 19. He said when he saw dem bring me here, he ran den and dare and asked Ole Mastah fo' me to marry him. You know, I told you he was born in Africa. Dey captured him and his mama whilest dey was out tendn' de field one day. He was only a young child when he got took from Africa. They sold his mama – yo' grand-mama – to some folks in a place called Georgia and he got sent over here to Texas.

But what he used to say was dat de pretty women in Africa would flirt wid de mens when courtn' time came. Hee! Hee! Hee! Now, yo' papa said I was actn' jess like I didn't wanna be bothered by him cauz I had so many other beaus seekn' my 'fection on dis plantation.

FLORENCE: Did you Mama? Have lots of other beaus?

MAMA:

I might' a turnt a eye or two. But nut'en like how yo' papa scribed yo' grand-mama. I never told you 'bout how her and yo' grand-papa met in Africa, did I? (*Florence shakes her head, pleased that she'd gotten her mama focused on a more pleasant subject*). Dis is how yo' papa always told me da story. She was said to be a mighty fine lookn' woman with a shape dat had mens coming from all over Africa. (*As they walk away and exit the stage engaged in conversation, African Dance Troupe approaches stage with "African Courtship Dance."*)

AFRICAN
COURTSHIP
DANCE:

(*This dance depicts the courtship of Florence's grand-parents and features authentic African dancers, drummers, and attire. The young village maiden is being pursued by a popular, good looking young village man. Although strongly attracted to him, she resists his advances before finally consenting to become his wife.*)

Inspired by Nimely Napla – Nimely Pan African Dance Company

(*Set stage for wooded area near Turner Plantation*)

Act Two

Scene Two

TIME:	One month later.
PLACE:	Wooded area near the Turner Plantation
MUSIC:	Instrumental; upbeat tempo.
LEWIS:	(*Lewis is walking; returning from Galveston Texas after handling business of selling Mastah Turner's cattle. He's on foot because his wagon broke down. He is approached by two Pattyrollers who check the roads for runaway slaves, making sure they have their "permission papers" to travel from one place to another.*)
DOUGLASS:	(*Pre-recorded or spoken not visible to audience*)
	He was a full-grown man now of 21 seasons. Full of dreams, love and a sense of freedom. His heart was like a volcano rupturing over with joy.

LEWIS: (*Exuberant*) Mr. Lincoln don' freed all of us. We's all free! I can marry Florence as soon as I gits home. I sure miss ya, Florence. She loves me! Why we might even have chiruns. Yes, dat's a good idea. Lots of chiruns! I's gon' buy us our own place. A place where we can look and see da land and da trees and all da beautiful birds. Ha! Ha!

DOUGLASS: Her eyes. He thought of her sparkling bright eyes and her pretty smile. He took out the kente cloth, held it to his heart then rubbed it against his cheek. So loud was his heart beating with joy, that he didn't even hear or see the slave-patrollers coming or "Pattyrollers" as they were called... until they had stopped him.

PATTY-
ROLLER #1: (*Staggering from drinking too much whiskey*). Well, Boy what you doing out here by yo'self so late?

LEWIS: My wagon broke down.

PATTY-
ROLLER #2: (*Been drinking, but being a thief, he's more focused than his companion*) Ain't you got no manners, Boy? You address us as "Sir."

LEWIS: Yes, Suh.

PATTY-
ROLLER #2:   Where's yo' pass anyhow? For all we
              know you could be a runaway.

LEWIS: I ain't no runaway. And 'sides dat Pres-
              ident Lincoln don' freed all us coloreds.
              (*Places the kente back in his pocket*).

PATTY-
ROLLER #1:   Freed! Boy you outta your mind? This
              is Grimes, Texas. Ain't nobody freed no
              niggas over here... (*Takes out his bottle,
              drinks a sip*) Never will. (*Passes bottle to
              companion – he takes a sip*).

LEWIS: Suh, y'all musta not heard da news. He
              don' signed dem papers! We's free to go
              as we please. Now if'n y'all excuse me. I
              gots to git on home. (*The necklace around
              Lewis' neck begins to heat up. He feels
              the strange heat, rubs his neck, but no
              relief comes*).

PATTY-
ROLLER #1:   (*Imitates in a mocking manner*)

              "If'n y'all excuse me, I gots to git on
              home." I guess you real anxious to get on
              home and tell everybody they's free, ain't
              you, boy?

DOUGLASS: (*Pre-recorded voice*) They wanted to
              lynch him then and there. Right on that
              dusty road.

PATTY-
ROLLER #1:   You know, I believe this here boy needs to be taught how we do things in Texas. We grow things big down here. Real big. Like trees. Come on boy. Let me show you what I'm talkn' about. (*They quickly seize Lewis. Begin to beat him. Patty-roller #2 checks Lewis' pockets and sees the cash, puts it into his own pocket Patty-roller #1 pulls out a rope. Enter Wade and Angus. They also see the Pattyroller take the money from Lewis' pocket*)

WADE: (*Speaking to the Pattyrollers*) What's going on here?

PATTY-
ROLLER #1:   We 'bout to have a Texas barbeque. Care to join us?

LEWIS: Mastah Wade, help me. Tell 'em to let me go. Mastah Wade!

PATTY-
ROLLER #2:   You know this boy? Is he one of yo' boys?

WADE: (*Studies the situation momentarily*) Never seen him in my life. But, I ain't got time for no party. We got business of our own to tend to. (*Pattyrollers exit stage with Lewis*).

ANGUS: We gon' just leave him back there, Wade? And the money? What about yo' papa's money?

WADE:

Shut up Angus! And you don't know nothing 'bout this, you hear me. Nothing! (*The two run away fast as they can*)

ANCESTOR
DANCERS:

(*Dance portrays the image of the lynching since audience does not really see the act take place. Male dancer assumes the spirit of Lewis conveying the agony of betrayal, injustice, suffering, and death, . Dance continues as Douglass speaks.*)

DOUGLASS:

(*Pre-recorded*). He cried out for help. But, mostly he cried out to God. And finally with his last breath, he thought of his love and uttered her sweet name. (*A brief pause*).

LEWIS:

FLO-RENCE!

DOUGLASS:

(*Pre-recorded*) Hung him by the neck until he died. To make mockery of him even further, they cut out his tongue. It was all about somebody's idea of what freedom meant – about privileges and about fears. Freedom is a spiritual situation. African people might have been chained and bound in shackles for almost 300 years, but some understood the meaning of true freedom. He knew.

MUSIC:

(*African Drumming is very powerful throughout this entire scene*)

YAA ASANTEWAA AND ANCESTOR CHILDREN:	(*Enter from backstage, but do not speak. Their movements are swift, breezy. With all the dancing about, Lewis makes a blending entrance from backstage with the same dance movements as the Ancestor Dancers. He is now wearing a white African robe with a long strip of kente cloth. He is greeted and then led by Yaa Asantewaa off the stage.*)
DOUGLASS:	(*Pre-recorded*). But even death could not kill his mission. He was destined to deliver a message. He heard the moans and cries of his enslaved people, praying "Kumbayah, my Lord, Kumbayah... oh Lord, come by here." He was given Divine permission to make way back to Texas and make a way for his people to become free. Now he was able to fly with the compassion of a dove, the wisdom of a raven and the strength of an eagle. The time had come for his people to be set free. And this time no man could hinder him. (*Briskly two Ancestor Dancers lead the procession up the aisle through the audience and out the rear entrance of the theater, followed by Yaa Asantewaa, then Lewis, then the Ancestor Children and finally the remaining ancestor Dancers. Drumming slows down and is lowered as Douglass speaks.*)

BLACKOUT.

ACT TWO

SCENE THREE

TIME: Two years later.

PLACE: Turner Plantation.

MUSIC: Instrumental; uplifting tempo.

                   (*All the Tellers; All the children including Stuart, Alice, Samuel, Luke, Ancestor Children can be in this scene as well. They are all sitting together in a gossiping circle.*)

TELLER #1:   (*Leans into the circle to tell this story so white folks outside of the circle won't be able to hear. Speaks almost in a whisper*) During the months dat passed, dey say some white people suddenly didn't feel right 'bout keeping slaves on day property cause dey felt owning them was bringn' on nothn' but bad luck. Some of dem white folks even moved off day own land, Child – for fear de Blacks wuz gon' re-volt and kill'em in the middle of de night!

LUKE: There sure was much talk about seeing birds in strange places. (*Begins to really make the story sound BIG.*) Sometimes there'd be birds seen up in the air and they were not even fly'n … just kind of perched up there on a cloud, lookn' like a stature or something!

SAMUEL: Some folks say dey often see a big eagle fly 'n 'round. Sometimes he perch his-self right on the peak of dat cliff. (*Points up to the cliff*). Say when he spreads out his wings, day stretch over a mile wide! (*Really makes the story big*)

LUKE: Oh, wow! You ever see him?

SAMUEL: Nawh! I'm jess telln' you what dey say?

ALL: OOOOOOOWWWWW!

ALICE: (*Eager to tell this part*) One day, Little Samuel was down playn' in da thickets where he "wuz not" suppose to be. Dey say a big 20-foot snake wrapped dat boy up and was 'bout to swallow him up whole…

TELLER #2: …Say dat big eagle swooped down from da sky and dug his claws into dat snake and tossed it up in de air and sliced it into mince meat. (*Shows listeners with exaggerated movement of arms the size of the eagle, the action of the snake wrap, and the toss. Make the story big!*)

TELLER #1:   Oooh! Do tell!

TELLER #2:   Saved dat silly boy!

ALICE: Bet he learned his lesson dat day, didn't he?

TELLER #2:   Sho did, Girl. He never did go back down dare in dem thickets again! *(All look at Samuel and laugh)*

ABBY: Then there was my cousin, Florence. One day she was all by herself gathering up the eggs and that scary Young Mastah Wade sneaked upon her. He decided... well I can't say this loud in front of the little children, but... *(She leans in and speaks to the older ones in a whisper)* it was time to teach Florence who her Mastah was gon' be. He didn't wanna wait no longer for her to show him some "affection". It wuz time she learn how to respect his authority. But, jess when he got ready to take advantage of that innocent girl...

SAMUEL: ...Dey say, de thunder began to clatter, *(Abby and older youth look startled that the younger ones know of these private matters)*

DANIEL: De lightn' began to flash and de wind picked Mastah Wade up and flung him into da river.

ALICE: Guess it musta washed his sins away cause he never went near Floey again!

TELLER #3:   (*An Older Girl*)

As Florence was walking back towards the house, she noticed an eagle flying over her heard. Like a shadow, if she slowed down, it slowed down. If she sped up, it flew faster. Soon she realized the bird was following her. Then something fell from its claws. (*Abby and Teller #3 begin gathering up the children sitting on the floor and start directing them off stage as she tells the story*).

ABBY: She watched as the bright colored kente cloth landed by her feet. Recognizing it immediately, she carefully picked it up and held it close to her heart. Then she rubbed it 'ginst her cheek. The eagle perched itself on a tall hill nearby. (*Tellers all exit as Abby's voice fades out with story.*)

CHILDREN: What happened to Floey? What happened to Floey? (*All are off stage. Florence enters*)

FLORENCE: (*In a very solemn mode. It's been two years since Lewis died; she sits on the tree stump, sings a chant.*)

Freedom, Freedom ©
By Ben Mboya Ward)

Freedom.   Freedom.   Ohhhhhh freedom.
Freedom.   Freedom.   Ohhhhhh freedom.

You've got your freedom now, Lewis. But, why did you have to die? I still think about you, Lewis. I know you've been protecting us from harm. But, it ain't like having you here with us – with me. And what about freedom? Looks like we always gon' be slaves. I know you believed freedom was gon' come. But, it sho' don't seem like it unless – unless you die. I see why it's easy for some not to believe in the spirits of the Ancestors because many of our people have lost hope. They've lost sight of where they came from so long ago. But, some of us will never forget. I'll never forget you, Lewis and your belief in freedom for all of us.

(*Lewis appears off to the side wearing a white flowing elegant African robe and hat. He stands and observes Florence as she speaks. He reaches for her but realizes she cannot see him. Somehow she must be made to feel his presence in order to restore her hope and faith. He steps forwards, drops the kente cloth in front of her as though it fell from the sky. Florence is startled, kneels down, picks up the cloth, holds it to her heart.*)

Is that what you're trying to tell me – that one day freedom will come to us all? (*Florence begins to cry. Lights rise brightly on her as sign of a powerful revelation. Florence then places the kente stole around her shoulders.*)

FLORENCE: Oh thank you, Lewis! Thank you! (*She sings reframe of "Love Will Find Away." This time she sings with gladness, then happily she runs off stage.*)

MUSIC: (*Instrumental continues "Love Will Find A Way."*)

ACT TWO

SCENE FOUR

TIME: Three Days Later.

PLACE: Turner Plantation.

MUSIC: Snare drums play marching tune.

REV. CLEO: (*Rev. Cleo runs out on stage calling all to come out; all slave characters come out. Douglass stands on the side in observance*)

                 Everybody, come on out here. Hurry up and git out here. Everybody! (*Mama, Florence, Abby, all the children, everyone come out.*)

SAMUEL: Time for Hambone Rev. Cleo?

REV. CLEO: Nawh, Samuel, this is far better blessn' dan Hambone. (*Laughs*)

                 Is everybody out here? Let Mama sit down so she can hear dis.

MAMA: What's going on Rev. Cleo?

REV. CLEO: Listn' careful y'all. Dis be mighty im-por-tant. I was jess in town wid Old Mastah Wade and all de folks wuz gathered to hear a man named General Gordon Granger talk. Remember dat name now y'all. What did I say his name was?

SEVERAL
CHILDREN: General Gordon Granger.

REV. CLEO: Yes. Dat be right. General Gordon Granger.

ALICE: What did he say Rev. Cleo?

REV CLEO: Just hold on a minute, little one. Just hold on.

(*Preparing to make the story impressive Rev. Cleo stands straight, clears his throat*). First of all he rode in on a biigg-ggg horse wearing a fancy blue uniform. He started by telling da people, how da war was over.

MAMA: Da war? Over?

REV CLEO: Yes'em been over for a few months now. But dar's more news. BIG news!

DANIEL: Well tell us Rev. Cleo!

REV CLEO: I's git'n to it! I's git'n to it! (*Pauses*)

Dis General Gordon Granger started readn' a special paper and it went somethn' like dis. I don't member every single word but I sho' member de important part. (*Clears his throat again*)

"Citizens across da State of Texas: I, General Gordon Granger, am appalled over da rumors of da happenings here. It is June 19, 1865. It's been over two years since our President, Abraham Lincoln, signed de *Emancipation Proclamation* freeing all Coloreds in dis country relieving dem of slave status. You have purposely rebelled against de authority of de United States. For Dis, you will have to be judged by God accordingly. (*Pauses*)

Now dis is da good part…he said (*Clears his voice again*)

"Beginning dis very day, all slaves is to be set free."

MAMA: What did you say Rev. Cleo? Did you say…?

REV. CLEO: Dat's right. He said "set free". He went onto say, "You is also to give dem accommodations whilst dey tran-sition demselves." Now dis is da part I really like, "If dey choose to remain on yo' property as workers, you is to compensate dem for da labor."

ABBY: Compensate? What do that mean Rev. Cleo?

FLORENCE: Pay. It means to get paid. Rev. Cleo…are you sure? Did he really say we're free?

REV. CLEO: Yes, Floey, we's free. Y'all wanna here da rest of what he said?

ALL: Yes Suh!

REV. CLEO: (*Clears his throat*) "Take heed. Any further selling, beating or killing of Coloreds is illegal. Anybody who continue to do so will be judged in de Court of law and, if convicted, shall face death! You can take my word for it!" Everybody…WE's ALL FREE!

ALL: (*All make shouts of joy and freeze*)

DOUGLASS: *(Steps on stage where the group is in freeze position; looks at them with joy)*

What General Gordon Granger neglected to tell the good folks was that he had no choice but to make this visit to Texas and other areas that still held Negroes in captivity. You see, he was headed North to give a report on the warfare, when out of "nowhere", he received orders to turn immediately and head down to Texas. Well, you can figure that one out for yourself. *(Pulls out a piece of kente cloth and looks at it with a smile)*

After General Gordon Granger spoke that day, word did get around to all who needed to hear the news about freedom. Over 250,000 Black people who were still in bondage, were freed. For them, humiliation had been internalized by hope. A wretched situation had been endured by faith. Men, women and children, though separated and treated like animals, survived gallantly like warriors, kings and queens.

MUSIC: (*African music combined with instrumen-
                  tals play Kumbaya as actors come out of
                  pose and run off stage with cheers. Every-
                  one is off stage but Douglass. Music fades
                  down. From this point on, each actor
                  comes out, says his/her line and remains
                  on stage. This gets all actors out on stage
                  for curtain call. Lines may be distributed
                  at Director's discretion. Communities may
                  wish to add their own personal Juneteenth
                  History*)

Act Two

Scene Four B

OPTIONAL: This scene can be used instead of previous scene. Or can be edited in a way to use both. Leave to Director's discretion. If the latter, additional time will be needed.

TIME: Two and a half years after Lewis was lynched.

PLACE: Galveston, Texas…where citizens and legislators have gathered to hear an important mandate from the President.

MUSIC: Snare drums play marching tune.

GENERAL
GORDON
GRANGER: (*Granger stands on stage and addresses
                audience as he states General Order #3;
                Douglass looks on from side*)

"Citizens across the State of Texas: I, General Gordon Granger, am appalled over the rumors of the happenings here. It is June 19, 1865. It's been over two years since our President, Abraham Lincoln, signed the Emancipation Proclamation freeing all Coloreds in this country relieving them of slave status. You have purposely rebelled against the authority of the United States. For this, you will have to be judged by God accordingly. Beginning this very day, all slaves are to be set free. You are also to give them accommodations while they transition themselves. If they choose to remain on your property as workers, you are to compensate them for their labor. Take heed. Any further importation, selling, beating or killing of Coloreds is illegal. Those who continue to do so will be judged in the Court of law and, if convicted, shall face death. You can take my word for it!"

(*Exits stage*)

DOUGLASS: (*Steps on stage where Granger made speech*)

What General Gordon Granger neglected to tell the good folks was that he had no choice but to make this visit to Texas and other areas that still held Negroes in captivity. You see, he was headed North to give a report on the warfare, when out of "nowhere", he received orders to turn immediately and head down to Texas. Well, you can figure that one out for yourself. (*Pulls out a piece of kente cloth and looks at it with a smile*)

After General Gordon Granger spoke that day, word did get around to all who needed to hear the news about freedom. Over 250,000 Black people who were still in bondage, were freed. For them, humiliation had been internalized by hope. A wretched situation had been endured by faith. Men, women and children, though separated and treated like animals, survived gallantly like warriors, kings and queens.

ALL: (*Cheer*)

MUSIC: (*African music combined with instrumentals play "Kumbaya." Everyone is off stage except Douglass. Music fades down. Off stage all actors prepare to enter for Epilogue which also serves as Curtain Call*)

EPILOGUE

TIME: Present Day

PLACE: Theater

*(Each cast member comes out, says his/
her line and remains on stage. This gets
all actors out on stage for Curtain Call.
Lines may be distributed at Director's
discretion. Communities may wish to add
their own personal Juneteenth History)*

LEROY: In lieu of celebrating July 4th as a day of
independence, the Negroes in Texas began
commemorating June 19th as their day of
Emancipation in 1865.

UNCLE EARL: It would take awhile before a bill would be
adopted and passed by the United States
Senate declaring June 19th as "Juneteenth
Independence Day." Actually it would be
132 years later in 1997.

LUKE: Kwanzaa too, is a celebration that was
not acquired overnight. Dr. Martin Luther
King, Jr. Holiday is still being rejected by
some states.

ALICE: But, still, Black people continue to press onward. It is that ongoing resurgence of Black consciousness and pride that gives Juneteenth the visibility it deserves.

DOUGLASS: "If there is no struggle...there is no progress."

ANCESTOR #1: In over 200 cities, Juneteenth has now become a celebration of African American history served on a soulful platter of down-home heritage which traces its roots back to the Motherland of Africa.

PROFESSOR
MANKATA: During the last week in July of each year, Ghana, West Africa commemorates its day of Emancipation from the British Colonies in 1957 in the same spirit as African Americans celebrate Juneteenth.

TELLER #3: Right here in the State of Minnesota, on March 27, 1996, the governor, enacted into law a bill that stated:

SAMUEL: June 19th is designated Juneteenth in recognition of the historical pronouncement of the abolition of slavery on June 19, 1865, when the *Emancipation Proclamation* was said to have been first publicly read in Texas.

ANCESTOR #2: The governor may take any action necessary to promote and encourage the observance of Juneteenth and public schools may offer instruction and programs on the occasion.

REV. CLEO: We were taken from our fields…

ALL: Yes!

REV. CLEO: Our homes…

ALL: Yes!

REV. CLEO: Our thrones…

ALL: Yes!

Rev. Cleo: Our families…

ALL: Yes!

REV. CLEO: For once we were all free!

ALL: Yes!

REV. CLEO: We toiled…

ALL: Yes!

REV. CLEO: We suffered…

ALL: Yes!

REV. CLEO: We gave birth…

ALL: Yes!

REV. CLEO: We survived…

ALL: Yes!

REV. CLEO: Because we were always free!

DOUGLASS: "Power concedes nothing without a demand, it never did and it never will."

ABBY: Ole Mastah made a miraculous recovery. Nobody could believe it. Say, he saw a man in his dreams with wings that were white as snow.

ANCESTOR #3: Yet, his body was black. He had wings that draped down to the ground where two children stood right between his two big elegant protective wings.

WAITRESS: Say ole Mastah knew he had died and guessed he was in Heaven being greeted by Saint Peter until he woke up the next morning. . .

DANIEL: Dat's when he realized he musta been dream'n. But, he felt better dan he had in over 20 years. So much better dat he figured he'd been spared to do better by de Black folks. Say he gave each family he had owned dey own plot of land with a deed!

WADE: As for his son, Young Mastah Wade...

ALL: Well?

ANGUS: Well...dey say ever since dat day he washed up outta dat river, he been traveln' around preachn' da gospel and telln' people how dey'd best repent cause dare's nothing swifter dan de raft of God!

ALL: (*Laugh*)

MAMA: (*Angus walks out with her listening intensely*)

Oh, yes I remember the very first June-teenth Festival here in the Twin Cities. Ha! Ha! Started over in Oak Park Neighborhood Center in North Minneapolis, it did. Big crowd! 'Bout 150 people Umm, Uhh. There was music, some good folks, good poetry and some mighty good food.

DEACON: That was almost 40 years ago. My! My! Things certainly have grown a bit. The Festival kept getting bigger and bigger and bigger. Had to move it to a bigger place...

LINCOLN: (*Lincoln and Mary Todd Lincoln walk out together*) ...Theodore Wirth Park in North Minneapolis became that bigger place. For years over 30,000 people attended each year. Truly a day for family and community to celebrate.

FLORENCE: (*Lewis and Florence enter holding hands*)

Just about the time when I thought I was lost...

ALL: (*Spoken with great enthusiasm*) ...My dungeon shook and my chains fell off!

LEWIS: Ha! Ha! I said, Just about the time when I thought I was lost...

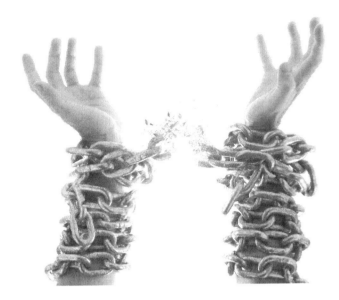

ALL: ...My dungeon shook and my chains fell off!

DOUGLASS: Jubilee done come! (*Steps away from the cast and moves down to the audience; speaks to them*)

Stepped on a pin, the pin bent and that's the way the story went! (*All grab hands, step forward and bow. exit stage, prepare for panel discussion after performance*).

THE END.

ACKNOWLEDGEMENTS

WMEP (West Metro Education Program), Minnesota Humanities Center, and Omaha Public Schools – thanks for supporting the revitalization of *Kumbayah...The Juneteenth Story* by introducing this history to more students, teachers, and community. Educational curricular can be enhanced as lesson units are redesigned to include this *absent narrative* (a term used by Minnesota Humanities referencing those voices and stories that tend to go unheard).

Belfry Books of Minneapolis and Jamaica Johnson, Austin, Texas, thanks for your publishing and graphics designs. I am deeply honored that award-winning visual artist, Christopheraaron Deanes of Minneapolis provided original images from his powerful collection along with youth artist, Angel Shock of Omaha, Nebraska. Steven Christopher Davis of Brooklyn Park, Minnesota – thank you for being the one in the audience allowed to take photographs.

Edie French and Paul Auguston of idream t.v. team in Minneapolis – thanks for capturing the videos and always exceeding our expectations. Eleanor Coleman, Minneapolis, Jennifer Tonko, Minnesota Humanities Center, Velma and Elmer Crumbley of Omaha, Nebraska – I appreciate your support and encouragement throughout this process. To Leroy Burns...love and miss you Dad.

In 1995, the collaboration between the Arts-Us Organization and the Twin Cities Juneteenth Committee began demonstrating how the arts could be used to teach critical omissions in history. Leola Seales, Chair of Twin Cities Juneteenth at the time, initiated the idea of developing a performance designed to help community understand the significance of the celebrated, yet undefined holiday. W. Toni Carter, Founder of Arts-Us was in total agreement. Thank you both for allowing me to exercise my artistic vision that led to the creation of *Kumbayah...The Juneteenth Story.*

Researching and developing the story's content became an incredible journey. I am so appreciative of the infinite wisdom of Qadi Mahmoud El-Kati. His mind-blowing brilliance took me on an educational adventure filled with inquiry: *How does he keep track of all this stuff? How did I not know this nor that not even that? Why is this not being taught in our schools?*

Stairstep Foundation and the Jerome Foundation attributed to Africa becoming more than just a mystical dream faraway. Thank you Alfred Babbington-Johnson, Menia Buckner, Al McFarlane, and Bobbie McFarlane for allowing me to participate in those life-altering immersion experiences to Ghana, West Africa.

My continued thanks to: Antar Saleem – Past-Director of Twin Cities Juneteenth, Delta Sigma Theta Sorority, Harvest Preparatory/SEED Academy, supporters from Rochester, Minnesota, Pilgrim Baptist Church, Ramsey and Hennepin County Libraries, Crosswinds East Metro Arts and Science School, Saint Paul Academy and Summit School, Minneapolis Public Schools, and Saint Paul Public Schools. Generous funding was made possible by General Mills Foundation, Target Corporation, East Metro Integrated School District and the Minnesota State Arts Board.

In the first edition of this publication, the original artwork and graphics were done by Shalette Cauley-Wandrick and manuscript editing by Alanna (Carter) Galloway and Shoshana Sagner of Saint Paul. Additional cultural research was contributed by Katherine Beecham of Roseville, Minnesota and Sandra Means of Rochester, Minnesota – thank you.

There was such excitement when *Kumbayah...The Juneteenth Story* was launched as an evening of storytelling and music held at Concordia University in Saint Paul. The high energy program featured the talented Arts-Us Young Storytellers and the Award Winning Excelsior Choir, Directed by Bobby Joe Champion. During the next nine months, tediously, a play was crafted. Over the next decade, astounding performances were held annually in beautiful spaces that included the Great American History Theatre, Concordia University's Beutow Memorial Music Hall, Pearson Theatre, and the Landmark Center's Weyerhaeuser Auditorium. Special event presentations or play excerpts began appearing on SPNN Television, MPS Education Channel, Mall of America, Hallie Q. Brown/Martin Luther King Center, Twin Cities Juneteenth Festivals, and Lucille's Kitchen. Tours included Herzl Camp in Webster, Wisconsin and Lambuth University in Jackson, Tennessee. I thank you Youth Performance Company for always being there for whatever we needed.

Youth! Youth! Youth! Thank God for them! Stacy Wilson, your clever high school project (that earned you an "A" of course) was awesome. You sewed each costume or found items in rummage sales – all on your own time. Through your self-determination, we no longer had to borrow costumes from other theater companies. To the Arts-Us Young Storytellers and Melissa (Logan) Mitchell, you all were my daily inspiration.

James A. Williams, I remain honored that you and W. Toni Carter were the first to take the words off paper and help the actors give them life. Later young Roslyn Harmon took the Director's helm. Our production was lifted even higher with the celebrity talents of Stephan Reynolds, now international dancer extraordinaire who went onto perform with Celine Dion, Michael Jackson, Broadway's The Lion King, Las Vegas' Cirque du Soleil's O, and more. Thank you celebrated vocalist, Mari Harris, renowned storyteller, Nothandu Zulu and award-winning actress, Edna Duncan. And the music! Thank you Ben Mboya Ward, Nimely Napla, Wilbert Dugas, Jamez Powell, Tom West, Frank Wharton, and Aaron James Bass. To Melvin Carter Jr. – thanks for the use of your Asante Stool each year (that you hand-carried all the way from Ghana to Saint Paul).

Our inaugural cast of children and teens are now adults doing outstanding work in their communities. To mention a few – Anthony Galloway – now leads school districts in understanding the importance of arts education and race matters; Metric Giles – is a firefighter in Saint Paul; Melvin Carter, III became a City Councilman in Saint Paul; Jesse Kanson-Benanav does urban planning in Boston; Will Shuford is an award-winning DJ, Jeremy McGee earned a full-ride in scholarships to MIT. To Adam Davis-McGee, Tenniece Nesbit, Suzie Shuford, Stormy Nesbit, Andrea Giles, Joselyn Hill, Isaiah Ellison, Ian Stevens, Antoinette Adjeia, Jeremiah Ellison, I am so proud of you. The original cast/program is included in this book. My apologies for any omissions.

Those who joined the production later include: Tashawn Moore, Tazia Edwards, Amani Ward, Michael Brooks, Marissa Rudd, Jonalyn Fair, Imani Belfrey-Waters, Rajel Johnson, Hannah Clark, Afyia Ward, Auston Clark, Michael Weah, Sam Kanson-Benanav, John Clark, Caleb Clark, Simone Johnson, Johnnie (Teddy Pendergrass Revue) Brown, Raymond Jackson, Jonathan Crockett, Ernest Simpkins, Idella McGrath, Isis McGrath, Thandizewe Jackson-Nisan, Julia Sewell, Kirby Maze, Kinsey Maze, Jesse Christensen, and special appearances by community leaders, Retired Judge Myron (Mickey) Greenwood and Jewelean Jackson..

Just as we have played and laughed over the years, there have also been heartaches and tears from the loss of loved ones in our production family. William "Billy" McGee, my greatest supporter and husband; my best friend, Linda Sesson Taylor, who personally made the food for our cast parties to ensure the children would get a "gourmet experience not cold cuts"; Brianna Lark, our sweet and funny girl; and Robert "Bobby" Hickman, the most serious among the cast. You are deeply missed A-Shay.

FORMER PRODUCTION MEMBERS *SHINING* EVEN BRIGHTER TODAY!

2009 Cast Members
Photographs by Steven Christopher Davis

What made Kumbayah unique – it was the first celebration of its kind that was created by the community to celebrate our history and educate our youth through theater. Rose McGee was light years ahead of her time. I'm glad I got to be a part of its inception.

—**James Austin Williams,** Actor/Director, Minneapolis, MN, Role: Production's First Director

The Kumbayah play made history come alive in the minds of my children. Their experiences as cast members provided a foundation of confidence and poise when speaking in public. We will always be grateful for Rose McGee and her passionate mentoring of young people!

—**Marcy Clark**, Parent Extraordinaire, Silver Spring, MD

Kumbayah was very eye opening for me. I learned a lot about something I hadn't been taught in school yet, which really helped me grasp the subject of African American history with new enthusiasm.

—**Simone Johnson**, 8th Grade, Dakota Hills Middle School, Minneapolis, MN Role: *Child Teller*

Even though there have been many strides in the U.S. since the June 19th, 1865, the play, Kumbayah, the Juneteenth Story still holds important resonance today as the struggle for full racial equality and justice continues in cities and communities across this country.

—**Jesse Kanson-Benanav,** Urban Planner, Boston, MA, Role: *Wade*

I learned of this historical production when bringing my daughters (birth & community) to the Arts Us Young Storytellers Summer Camp, which led to the next decade of involvement and support of this Annual Juneteenth play. This option contributed greatly to their personal development and becoming the phenomenal young women they are today. One year, when my birth daughter was injured playing hockey, my reality kicked in when I volunteered to stand in for her. She had gigantic shoes to fill. Needless to say, it was a landmark time in my life. Asante Sana

—**Ms. Jewelean Jackson**, Community Elder, National Ms. Kwanzaa, Minneapolis, Role: *Mama* (Stand-in)

Kumbayah is more than just a book or a play, it's more than just words on pages. It is an enriched learning experience that broadens one's horizon pertaining to African American culture. It will deepen your perspective on African American History. It is truly food for your soul that will stick with you for eternity. I'm just grateful to have been part of the experience.

—**Jazzalette Wandrick**, Saint Paul, MN, Role: *Child Teller, Florence*

The Kumbayah play has helped me to realize the struggles and sacrifices of my ancestors who have gone before me. As a result, I feel well prepared to run my race from a point of view projected off their shoulders.

—**John Clark** age 16, 11th Grade, Silver Spring, MD, Role: *Ancestor Child*

I was involved in Kumbayah for many years and the rhythmic lines of the script still ring in my head. Those were challenging lines that forced me to embody on stage a shameful history that removed me far from my comfort zone. Off stage I was energized working with a cast of such joyful and talented individuals that became the bedrock of my summer community.

—Sam **Kanson-Benanav**, Chef, Brooklyn, NY, Role: *Luke*

Rehearsing and performing in Kumbayah...The Juneteenth Story was the highlight of my summer as a youth. (true)

—**Jeremy McGee,** Technologist and Entrepreneur, San Francisco, CA, Role: *Ancestor Child*

As Director of Kumbayah for three years, this phenomenal production about the history of slavery and emancipation was the foundation for many of the performers (young and old) to discover their inner gifts, develop self-confidence, and acquire personal success! Rose McGee, the visionary behind this masterpiece, has paved the way for communities to learn and become educated by displaying what it means to embrace love, honor and freedom! Kumbayah is a significant catalyst for community restoration, hope and most importantly, TRUTH!

—**Roslyn Harmon**, Pastor, Circle of Healing Ministry, Minneapolis, MN, Role: Director

Kumbayah, holds a very special place in my heart! It reminds me of the importance of celebrating our freedom. In a time like today, where civil rights and human rights are still being challenged, it is ever more necessary! So, "Kumbayah dear lord, Kumbayah!" This story needs to be told year after year, until all men and women are treated equally! In the words of Frederick Douglass, "They must become educated!"

—**Stephan isijia Reynolds**, Dancer, Choreographer, Producer, Atlanta, GA, Role: Production's Choreographer, *Lead Ancestor Dancer*

This beautiful play combines the history of Ghana, West Africa with the sorrows of American slavery. Being a member of the cast had a profound impact on my cultural perspective.

—**Alston Clark**, Sophomore, Howard University, Washington, D.C., Role: *Daniel*

I grew up as a Kumbayah cast member starting at age nine. I may have set the record for the many different roles played by one person. Plus, I had the unique opportunity as a young teenager to help edit the first edition of the book. At age seventeen, we toured to Tennessee with a stop in Memphis. This was my first time traveling with a production company. While there, we visited the Lorraine Motel, where Rev. Dr. Martin Luther King, Jr. was assassinated. My positive experiences as a Kumbayah cast (family) member, both on the set and off, have shaped the person I am today, and will stay with me forever.

—**Alanna (Carter) Galloway,** Proud Mom, Steward/ CWA Local 7250, Saint Paul, Roles: *Alice, Abby, Florence, African Drum Ensemble,* Book Editor

Re-enacting history gave me a deeper understanding of the journey my ancestors braved. Learning to put myself in their shoes while I grew as a performance artist enriched by public speaking abilities and taught me to value my history more.

—**Hannah M. Clark**, Junior, Howard University, Washington, D.C., Role: *Alice*

This play provides a unique approach to our history that's often left out of mainstream curriculum. It's an intergenerational learning experience that connects the past and present as well oral and written narratives. This is an awesome tool that should be used throughout the creative arts and education landscape.

—**Adam Davis-McGee**, Multimedia Producer, Golden Valley, MN, Roles: *Samuel, Hambone Man, African Drum Ensemble*

Kumbayah…The Juneteenth Story visits a small Texas town, and the lives of children and families free in spirit though bound in the institution of slavery. It speaks into our lives the "sankofa" message: to seek and safeguard precious wisdom from the past to secure and build our future.

—**W. Toni Carter,** Ramsey County Commissioner, Saint Paul, MN, Role: Production Co-Director

I was lucky enough to be in the cast of Kumbayah starting in the seventh grade. Juneteenth is such a vital part of our history that I knew nothing about. I was able to learn it not in the classroom, but in community theatre. Thank you, Rose!

—**Arne Gjelten**, Actor, Los Angeles, CA, Role: *Stuart*

Juneteenth was where I began to understand dedication to something that could change the perspectives of actors and the audiences.

—**John Stephens**, Graduate Actor, Macalester College, Saint Paul, MN,   Role: *Ancestor Child*

Freedom is not a physical attribute; it's a state of mind.

—**TaShawn Moore,** Actor, North Hollywood, CA, Roles: *Professor Mankata, Yaa Asantewaa*

I entered the production of Kumbayah at a young age and was mesmerized by the writer's brilliant way of bringing a story to life. I worked with strangers that slowly became lifelong friends. I was part of the play and now the play will forever be a part of me.

—**Tazia Edwards** (aka) Hip-Hop Dancer, Saint Paul, MN, Roles: *Waitress, Lead Ancestor Dancer*

My experience in Kumbayah enabled me to learn the true meaning of Juneteenth and its significance to our people and this country, which I very well may not have learned had I not been involved. Lifelong relationships, friendships, and family ties were established. This production is a much needed work of art today especially given the current state of things in this country. Much of what I do now in music is a direct result of my experience as a child with the production of Kumbayah... The Juneteenth Story.

—**Will Shuford** (DJ Willi Shu), Music Producer, Minneapolis, MN, Role: *Daniel*

Some childhood memories are good, some are bad.... Kumbayah was an extraordinary positive childhood memory for me that lasted for several years. It was a pleasure and honor to serve while learning about key points in my ancestors' history. I still find myself reciting quotes from the play, "Stepped on the pin, the pin bent, and that's the way the story went." Mr. Hickman (rest his soul) was the heart of the play. I'll be forever grateful to Ms. McGee."

—**Thandisizwe Jackson-Nisan,** Community Servant Leader, Minneapolis, MN, Role: *Mama*

IN MEMORY OF OUR BELOVED STARS WHOSE WARMTH NOW RADIATES AS ANCESTOR ENERGY

William Earl (Billy) McGee, Chief Public Defender for Hennepin County, My #1 Fan d. Nov 13, 2000 at age 47

Linda Sesson Taylor, Attorney, Jackson, TN d. May 22, 2008 at age 57, Our Annual Cast Party Gourmet Cook

Brianna Lark (Samuella) d. Dec 19, 2012 at age 21

Robert (Bobby) Hickman (Frederick Douglass) d. Jan 28, 2015 at age 79

RESOURCES

idream t.v.
Promotional Video of *Kumbayah...The Juneteenth Story*
Video Production iDream.tv, Paul Auguston, Eddie French
Kevin Quinn, Ryan Melling, available to view on line at:
www.idream.tv/kumbayah

During the late 1990s when Kumbayah ...The Juneteenth
Story was first written, there was little to no curriculum
that addressed the history of Juneteenth. Thanks to the ever
increasing popularity of the Internet, today more resources
are accessible that offer quality lesson units. Anyone can
click right onto several reputable websites that provide
national calendar of events, podcasts, community gatherings
as well as historical documents.

Most of the lessons accessible online are very detailed and
applicable for grade levels 2-12 and include suggested books,
fun activities, essay questions, essay topics, quizzes, tests,
and chapter abstracts. For planning, there are worksheets,
evaluation forms and more. The following information comes
directly from two online resources who gave permission to
be listed in this publication of *Kumbayah..The Juneteenth
Story* - HotChalk and ReadWriteThink.

Hot Chalk
http://www.hotchalk.com/ HotChalk, Inc. 1999 S. Bascom
Avenue Suite 1020 Campbell, CA 95008

HotChalk

Sample Lesson Unit:
This is an end of the school year activity with a Juneteenth
Presentation Celebration. This lesson analyzes African
American folktales, songs, and hymns during the time of
slavery.

- This technology-based unit on slavery
  incorporates PowerPoint, a WebQuest,
  and Inspiration software.
- This PowerPoint lecture is titled "*On
  the Backs of Slaves.*"
- This is an "*Underground Railroad*"
  WebQuest.
- In "*Inspiration to Map Slavery,*"
  students chart the process of slavery
  including the Triangle Trade
  Route, regions of slavery, reasons,
  consequences, etc. using Inspiration
  software.
- In "*Path of a Slave,*" students make
  PowerPoint presentations mapping the
  journey of a slave from Africa to the
  Thirteen Colonies.

Links to Lesson Units:
- http://www.readwritethink.org/
  classroom-resources/calendar-
  activities/celebrate-juneteenth-20547.
  html
- http://www.lessonplans.
  com/?s=Juneteenth

- http://lessonplanspage.com/
  juneteenth-htm/
- http://www.crayola.com/lesson-plans/
  juneteenth-proclamation-jubilation-
  lesson-plan/

ReadWriteThink
http://www.readwritethink.org/ ReadWriteThink 800
Barksdale Road P.O. Box 8139 Newark, Delaware 19714-
8139
Sample Lesson Units Includes Books, Poems, and Study
Guides:

readwritethink

- Ralph Ellison's *Juneteenth*; Carolyn
  Meyer's *Jubilee Journey*; Ann
  Rinalidi's *Come Juneteeth*; *Juneteenth*
  by Mark Schroder; and *Juneteenth:
  A Day to Celebrate Freedom from
  Slavery* by Angela Leeper.
- These *Sweet Clara and the Freedom
  Quilt* lesson plans and links include
  an Interdisciplinary Unit (2-8), a
  geography and economics lesson (K-
  5), a language arts and social studies
  (1-2) lesson plan and Teacher Cyber
  Guide (3). This site also contains a
  Teacher's Idea Bank that includes
  links to other lesson plans on African
  American history and culture.
- A Juneteenth social studies lesson plan
  titled *Lift Every Voice and Sing*. (4)

- In this research lesson plan, students discover their community Juneteenth celebrations and create an educational advertising campaign about the local activities and traditions. The ideas of ownership and the impact of slavery are also covered. (4)
- Venn diagrams are used in this math lesson to compare Juneteenth and 4th of July.
- In this art lesson plan from Crayola, students make a replica of the Emancipation Proclamation.
- In this PBS Kids civics lesson activity, students research slavery and anti-slavery organizations that exist around the world today. They then develop an action plan to fight slavery and help current slaves gain their freedom. Although this is not a Juneteenth lesson plan, can you think of a more meaningful way to celebrate Juneteenth?
- A middle school lesson plan at History Now evaluates how different groups in American viewed the Emancipation Proclamation when it came out. It includes worksheets and character sheets to be filled out by each group.
- This EdSitement high school lesson plan explores the Emancipation Proclamation from an African American perspective and contains an extensive list of related materials.

A Synopsis of Juneteenth's History:
During the <u>US Civil War</u>, President <u>Abraham Lincoln</u> issued the <u>Emancipation Proclamation</u> on September 22, 1862, with an effective date of January 1, 1863. Although it declared that slaves were to be freed in the <u>Confederate States of America</u> in rebellion against the federal government, it had minimal actual effect. Even after the ending of military hostilities, as a part of the former Confederacy, Texas did not act to comply with the Emancipation Proclamation.

On June 19, 1865, <u>Union</u> General <u>Gordon Granger</u> and 2,000 federal troops arrived in <u>Galveston, Texas</u>, to take possession of the state and enforce the <u>emancipation</u> of its slaves. While standing on the balcony of Ashton Villa, Granger read the contents of "General Order No. 3":

June 19th has since become known as <u>Juneteenth</u>, a <u>portmanteau</u> of the words June and nineteenth. Former slaves in Galveston rejoiced in the streets with jubilant celebrations. Juneteenth celebrations began in Texas the following year.[5] Across many parts of Texas, freed people pooled their funds to purchase land specifically for their communities' increasingly large Juneteenth gatherings — including Houston's Emancipation Park, Mexia's Booker T. Washington Park, and Emancipation Park in Austin.

The event was made a Texas state holiday beginning in 1980, under legislation introduced by freshman Democratic state representative Al Edwards. The legislation was opposed by African-American representative Clay Smothers of Dallas County, who declared the holiday "fraudulent" and belittled the observance as merely "ceremoniously grinning and bursting watermelons on the Capitol grounds." Juneteenth is a "partial staffing holiday", meaning that state offices do not close, but some employees use a floating holiday to take the day off. Schools are not impacted because they are already into summer vacation by June 19.

Its observance has spread to many other states, with a few celebrations taking place even in other countries. As of May 2013, 43 U.S. states and the District of Columbia have recognized Juneteenth as either a state holiday or special day of observance; these are Alabama, Alaska, Arkansas, California, Colorado, Connecticut, Delaware, Florida, Georgia, Idaho, Illinois, Indiana, Iowa, Kansas, Kentucky, Louisiana, Maine, Maryland, Massachusetts, Michigan, Minnesota, Missouri, Nebraska, Nevada, New Jersey, New Mexico, New York,[North Carolina, Ohio, Oklahoma, Oregon, Pennsylvania, Rhode Island, South Carolina, Tennessee, Texas, Vermont, Virginia, Washington, West Virginia, Wisconsin, and Wyoming.

In 1996 the first legislation to recognize "Juneteenth Independence Day" was introduced in the U.S. House of Representatives, H.J. Res. 195, sponsored by Barbara-Rose Collins (D-MI). In 1997 Congress recognized the day through Senate Joint Resolution 11 and House Joint Resolution 56. In 2013 The U.S. Senate passed Senate Resolution 175, acknowledging Lula Briggs Galloway (late president of the National Association of Juneteenth Lineage) who "*successfully worked to bring national recognition to Juneteenth Independence Day*", and the continued leadership of the National Juneteenth Observance Foundation.

Other References:

Sarpong, P. (1971). *The sacred stools of the akan*. Ghana, W. Africa: Ghana Publishing Corp.

El-Kati, M. (2009). *The hiptionary*. Saint Paul, MN: Papyrus Publishing Inc.

Lincoln, A. (1863) *Emancipation Proclamation*. Washington D.C.   *http://www.abrahamlincolnonline.org/lincoln/ speeches/emancipate.htm.*

Granger, G. (1865) *General Order #3*. Galveston, TX *http:// nationaljuneteenth.com/General_Order.html*

Notes

Notes

FEATURED ARTIST

Christopheraaron Deanes

Original Works Featured:
Cover: *Praying Hands With Kente Shadow* – Oil, Gesso, Rice on Wood
All To Thee – Oil, Gesso, Rice on Wood
To The Hills – Oil, Gesso, Rice on Wood

Christopheraaron Deanes develops narratives that depict communities engaged in social, religious and political works while holding true to each one's own identity and engagement of others. He is a graduate of the Minneapolis College of Art and Design in Graphic Design, has a Master's Degree in Curriculum and Instruction from the University of Saint Thomas, and holds Educational Certification from Saint Mary's University of Minnesota. He works with Minneapolis Public Schools and is with the John T. Biggers Seed Project – a public arts venture with the City of Minneapolis Public Works and the University of Minnesota's Urban Research Department.

Made in the USA
San Bernardino, CA
13 September 2015